M000159324

De-stressing 101: Tools for Living a Stress-Free Life

The Course You Were Never Taught in School

By

Dr. Karen Dja Ashby

www.DiscoverInnerPeace.com

Sema Books
P.O. Box 570459
Miami, Florida, 33257
Phone: (305) 378-6253 Fax: (305) 378-6253

Second U.S. edition © 2006 By Dr. Karen Dja Ashby

Ashby, Dr. Karen Dja
De-stressing 101: Tools for Living a Stress-Free Life
ISBN: 1-884564-59-3

Library of Congress Cataloging in Publication Data

SEMA INSTITUTE

www.DiscoverInnerPeace.com

Author Biography

Karen Dja Clarke-Ashby was born in Guyana, South America. Her family moved to the United States in 1974. She grew up and still resides in Miami, Fl. She has a doctoral degree in the medical sciences.

Dr. Ashby is a certified Yoga Exercise instructor. She lectures on the health and stress management applications of Yoga for modern society. She is a Pastoral Health, Nutrition and Spiritual Counselor, as well as an independent researcher, practitioner and teacher of Integral Yoga Systems. She is a Yoga Life-style Consultant. She is a Doctor of Veterinary Medicine. She received her veterinary degree from the University of Florida College of Veterinary Medicine, where she graduated with honors.

Dr. Ashby is also the author of *Happiness 101: The Course You Were Never Taught in School*, co-author of "*The Egyptian Yoga Exercise Workout Book*," and a contributing author for "*The Kamitan Diet, Food for Body, Mind and Soul*."

DEDICATION

This book is dedicated to my niece, Kay-Vibhuti, because I feel, the best gift family elders can give their children, nieces, nephews is advice/wisdom/guidance about life, based on the lessons they learned in their own lives, in relation to living a well-lived life and avoiding the unnecessary hardships of life.

A spiritual teacher once said:

Experience is the best teacher for fools...the wise learn by observation!

So, my dear niece, be wise and learn from my experiences and observations!

If you are able to learn the valuable techniques of de-stressing presented in this book, not only will you have a better quality of life, but you will also have an opportunity to accomplish great things in your life. And imagine how much more of a positive impact you will have on the world, because you will be able to start sharing this with others even from your young age.

By the time you become an adult, you will be so wise, as will your cousins and friends who are able to observe you and learn from you. And, with wisdom, comes something just as special, as stated in this ancient proverb:

Be Wise and You Will Be Happy!

I would like to thank my husband,
Dr. Reginald Muata Ashby
for his editorial and technical assistance,
and unceasing support.

I would like to thank my spiritual teacher
for sharing his wisdom on
and being an example of
how to live a stress-free life.

I would like to thank my parents
and other family members,
including my mother-in-law,
for their suggestions, editorial assistance,
and unceasing support over the years.

I would also like to thank Uncle Ray and Sesheta for reading
the manuscript, and for their suggestions and editorial
assistance.

A thank you also goes to O. Reid for the drawings of the
respiratory and digestive systems.

TABLE OF CONTENTS

Introduction

I had mentally written portions of this book over the years out of my desire to help family, friends, and co-workers when they are stressed out. However, the final inspiration to put it in writing came from my niece. She lives in a different town, several hours from where I live. I had called her to see how she was doing. She was not available, so I spoke to her mother. Her mother began to explain to me that my niece had a very difficult week, because of intense testing/exams at school. She explained to me that my niece was unable to complete one of her tests, because she had such a headache she could no longer think. Also, during the period of testing, she had no appetite for breakfast, and then, after the tests, had intestinal cramps. What she was describing to me were signs that I knew all too well, from personal experience as well as my research...signs of stress. The exams had caused my niece to become stressed out. I briefly discussed with her mother about stress, the effects of stress, and how to counter these effects. After I got off the phone, I realized that my discussion with her mother was still very incomplete and therefore limited, and sat down and began to write this book.

We generally associate stress with adults who have "real" problems, but more and more children, youths and young adults are facing issues that they may not be emotionally equipped to handle. Therefore, they are very susceptible to stress, and becoming stressed out, especially if they do not know how to effectively de-stress. In addition, studies show that these stressful episodes may predispose them to serious health conditions as adults[1]. One medical study funded by the National Heart, Lung and Blood Institute found that young adults who experienced large increases in their blood pressure due to the effects of psychological stress were more likely to develop hypertension (high blood pressure) when they reached middle aged.[2] Therefore, parents and guardians need to be able to recognize signs of stress in their child(ren), and to model and teach them healthy and effective ways of de-stressing. But even more important, young people should be informed about stress and de-stressing as well; they should know the signs of stress so they can recognize when they are becoming stressed out, as well as what they can do to prevent, eliminate and recuperate from stress in a healthy and effective way.

So, this book is recommended for youths, young adults and adults, because the habit we have of being stressed out as adults is just a progression of how we learned to react to life's situations as children. So, we generally learn the habit of being stressed out very early in life, and then continue to "perfect" the stressed out way of handling life's difficult and challenging situations as we grow older. It is no wonder that most adults experience stress on a regular basis. By the time we are adults, we have had so much time practicing it, that it can become an automatic response…a habit.

In addition, because the effects of stress are not benign and the habit of becoming stressed out is a learned behavioral response that usually takes root early in life, it would seem that it should be mandatory for schools to teach courses on de-stressing as a part of life skills. However, this is not yet a widespread practice (hence the subtitle of this book, *The Course You Were Never Taught In School*), even though the grades of the students would improve if such courses were implemented. Students would miss less schooldays from being ill due to stress-related illnesses, especially illnesses that result from or are associated with a suppressed immune system, such as colds and the flu. In addition, they would enjoy better health later on in life.

Because becoming stressed out is a learned behavioral response to dealing with life situations that are often difficult and challenging, it can be un-learned. It can be replaced with healthy learned responses, such as the techniques presented in this book, which include seeking counseling or assistance from peers or professionals who are knowledgeable in whatever area you are facing your difficulty.

Many people do not seek the assistance of professionals when they are experiencing a difficult or challenging situation. Oftentimes they do not want to spend the money to do so. However, their lack of experience and knowledge in a particular area can lead to faulty decision making and inappropriate actions that can further complicate their circumstances and create more stress, and may end up costing them more financially in the end.

In addition, being bogged down in indecision and confusion and not having the facts about one's options or not having clear insight into what options are available is in itself stressful. Many people try to make decisions about a particular situation without knowing all the facts, and don't even realize this is why they become stuck in indecision and confusion. If one does not have all the facts about a situation to weigh the pros and cons of a particular action, making an effective, informed and calm decision is going to be difficult, if not impossible. So, consider consulting professionals in whatever areas you are experiencing difficulties…for your mental, physical, and likely, your financial wellbeing.

If there are difficulties in a relationship (a broken down relationship), most people do not seek relationship counseling. However, if their car were to break down, they would take it to a professional car service person to repair it. If they want to get a haircut, they go to a hair-cutting professional. So, if you are experiencing stress due to a financial matter, in addition to practicing de-stressing techniques, why not seek assistance from a financial counselor. If you are experiencing stress due to a relationship problem, in addition to practicing de-stressing techniques, how about seeking assistance from a relationship therapist. If you are having problems with schoolwork, in addition to practicing de-stressing techniques, why not seek assistance from a tutor. If it is a legal matter, many lawyers offer a free initial consultation that can provide you with insight on how best to proceed.

As human beings, we need other human beings to teach us and show us the way. From the day we were born, this is how we learned, and the more expertise the person teaching us had in that particular area, the more effective and efficient it made the learning process. The other way humans learn is by trial and error, or the school of hard knocks...which at times can knock us pretty hard! So, seeking assistance from professionals to increase your proficiency in a particular area is not a sign of weakness, but a sign of being human, and can go a long way to relieving your stress.

And the same applies for stress...rather than suffer from its effects, why not seek assistance from experts who can assist you in releasing, preventing and eliminating stress from your life. Reading this book is taking an important step towards empowering yourself by becoming proficient at de-stressing, because it will show you how and why it is possible for you to control if you become stressed out or not.

However, be sure to follow through on the techniques and recommendations that require you to seek assistance in different areas if these areas are an essential part of your de-stressing program, such as from a counselor, yoga exercise teacher, stress-management teacher/counselor, psychologist, tutor, support group, pastoral counselor, financial advisor, lawyer, realtor, etc., without hesitation.

Why is it so important to learn to handle and prevent stress? So you can enjoy a better quality of life, be happier, and be healthier, physically and mentally. Who does not want to experience peace of mind and happiness in life? Everyone is seeking just that, and de-stressing is the most basic and effective way to accomplish it, because if one is stressed out, then even the usual activities that normally cause one to feel happy will no longer do so. Most people do not want to be around family or friends when they are stressed out; they usually just want to be left alone. Even food or other pleasures are not enjoyable or enjoyable to the same degree when one is stressed out. So stress affects the very quality of life, and for the worse, rather than for the better.

In the short term, and more so in the long term, the stressed out way of handling life's difficulties can have a very detrimental effect on one's health, some with even deadly consequences. Many of the most common health conditions that plague our society such as headaches, gastrointestinal problems (e.g., ulcers, colitis), fatigue, insomnia, depression, high blood pressure, high cholesterol, heart disease, heart attacks, cancer, immune problems, etc., have been associated with or are caused by stress.

If you had no choice but to be stressed out, that is one thing. But you do have a choice and can do something about it, so why not? Why not improve your quality of life, and enjoy life more?

When you understand that stress is not so much about what is going on outside around you, but inside, within your body-mind complex, then you can begin to de-stress, because although you may not be able to control what is going on around you, with practice and training, you can control much of what is going on in your mind and how that manifests in your emotions.

And why should you make de-stressing a priority in your life? Well, in addition to feeling better emotionally, de-stressing can also improve your physical health, and even possibly save your life.

I have provided references, including medical and scientific references, for several topics of discussion in this book as footnotes or endnotes. I encourage you to read these. In some instances, I included a brief excerpt (quote) from the actual reference immediately after the bibliography to show how the reference supports the point that is being discussed. I have also provided a list of resources in the back of this book to support your process of effectively de-stressing, based on the tools presented in this book.

Part 1: Understanding Stress

Chapter 1: Role Of The Stress Response In Becoming Stressed Out

The Stress Response is a Good Thing?

Yes, the Stress Response is a VERY good thing, that is, when the Stress Response is used as it was designed to be used. The Stress Response is a survival mechanism that human beings have to allow them to react to life-threatening situations. It is also called the "Fight or Flight Response." In other words, this response allows us to either be able to fight off some life-threatening danger (fight response), or run away from the life-threatening danger (flight response).

So, the Stress Response is actually a natural and good thing! In life or death situations, we need the Stress Response to help us to survive. Without it, we would have a greater likelihood of dying in life-threatening, life or death situations.

Therefore, the Stress Response is a survival mechanism that your mind-body complex has to try to save your life when you are faced with a life or death situation, such as if you were in the zoo and a lion escaped and were facing you right now, licking his lips as he is ready to pounce on you and eat you. Even without your thinking about it, your Stress Response would kick in and cause all sorts of biological, physiological and hormonal changes in your body[1] so you could either run away from the lion, or try to fight it off....to survive.

> The Stress Response (SR) Is a Survival Mechanism In Life Or Death Situations.

It would also be a good thing for your Stress Response to become activated if you were seriously injured in a car accident...again, a life-threatening, life or death situation.

---

[1] We will discuss these changes more in depth later on.

Without the Stress Response activating in such situations, your chances of surviving would be reduced.

Stress and Handling the Practical Realities of Life

Handling one's practical realities of life refers to handling the normal ups and downs, prosperities and adversities, and different situations and challenges or problems that everyday life brings...that are not life-threatening, that are not a matter of life or death.

One's practical realities can always be handled in two ways, from a state of calmness, or from a state of emotionality (fear or anger – i.e., stress). Regardless of how you choose to approach and handle each situation, being calm or being upset, the situation gets handled. But one way you are a nervous, stressed out wreck, and the other way you are calm and energized.

Becoming Stressed Out: Activating the Stress Response for a False Alarm

When we become upset and afraid, and overreact to a problem or challenge in life that is not a matter of life or death as if it is a matter of life or death, and make a big deal about it, our body thinks we are in big trouble, that we are in a life or death situation, and the Stress Response automatically becomes activated.

Therefore, when we are not careful about controlling our emotions, we set off false alarms in the Stress Response.

The effects of a false alarm activation of the Stress Response are what people are experiencing when they say they are "stressed out." A test in school is not a life or death situation. Failing a test is not a life or death situation. You may face certain consequences because you failed the test, such as taking it over, doing extra credit work, being grounded by your parent(s), not getting a promotion, etc., but these are also not a matter of life or death. You will survive these challenges whether you fail or succeed. You will also have a better chance of succeeding if you can stay calm and do not become stressed out, because when you become stressed out, it is more difficult to think clearly.

When we are not careful about controling our emotions, we set off false alarms in the SR and become stressed out.

Your brother or sister doing something to annoy you is not a life or death situation. Having someone say something nasty to you is not a life or death situation. Being late for school or work is not a life or death situation.

Even situations that can cause us to have many difficulties such as losing one's job and not being able to pay the rent or mortgage, or even losing one's home, are not life or death situations. They may cause us to have to make changes in our lives, sometimes very drastic changes such as going to live with a family member if we were to lose our home, but they are NOT life or death, life-threatening situations...such as a lion being ready to eat you right now, or being in a really bad car accident where you could actually die.

> You may be facing a difficult situation and may even need to see a counselor for help, but if it is not a life or death situation, you don't need your SR activated.

Life is change. For many people, change = stress. Change can evoke anxiety and fear about what the future may bring. Consequently, situations that involve big life changes such as the death of someone close, moving, or divorce can cause many people to feel overwhelmed, and become stressed out. For others, just getting out of bed in the morning to face life is stressful; they become overwhelmed with fear and anxiety about what they may face that day. Moreover, even when the change is in favor of the individual (a prosperous condition), just the change itself triggers stress. Furthermore, there is additional stress from worrying about or wondering when the good times (prosperous conditions) are going to end.

> Because life = change, resisting change means resisting the unfoldment of life.

Resisting change and becoming stressed out by it is in effect resisting the unfoldment of life itself. But understandably, some situations life brings are certainly more difficult to cope with than others. The death of a family member is certainly one of the more difficult situations to handle, but still, it is not a matter of life or death for the person grieving. In fact, death is a normal part of life...one of life's situations that must be faced by all with respect to oneself, as well as family, friends, acquaintances, and even strangers. However, one may not have the coping skills or a philosophy of life to allow one to handle the situation with calm.

Still, the answer is not to settle for a life of becoming very emotionally distraught and stressed out, because being stressed out can have some serious health consequences. In other words, becoming stressed out is not just a matter of letting off steam. It is not a benign process. There is a physiological price to be paid when the Stress Response is triggered. In a true life or death situation, that physiological price is a small pittance to pay for one's survival. However, in a situation that is not life or death, that price can be pretty high; it can even have deadly consequences because stress can cause and is associated with numerous conditions of ill health.

> Letting off steam is not a benign process; there is a physio- logical price to pay when the SR is activated.

Unfortunately, courses on coping strategies are not generally taught in school, and as the complexity of life has increased in modern times, more and more people just do not know how to cope with or handle life's situations, or the mistakes they make when trying to handle life's practical realities.

However, rather than allowing yourself to be overwhelmed by life's situations that are not a matter of life or death, seek to acquire the tools necessary for de-stressing, including counseling, psychological and or spiritual, which will allow you to gain insight into and develop skills for handling the ever changing situations that are a normal part of life. Applying the de-stressing techniques that you will learn in this book will greatly facilitate this process of handling the practical realities of normal, every day life.

Wealth Does Not Equal Freedom From Life's Challenges

Some people wrongly think if they were wealthy, they would be free from life's challenges, but this is not correct. It is naive to think this way. Wealthy people have their own challenges to face, some related to being famous or wealthy (lack of privacy, difficulty in having sincere relationships with others, etc.), and others related to just being human (illness, family problems, divorce, death of loved ones, issues from their childhood such as abuse, etc.). Look at how many rich and famous personalities have overdosed on drugs. Why did they take drugs in the first place? Because they did not know how to cope with their problems, their life situations, and perhaps even their success. So, yes, even the rich and famous have problems, and they too eventually learn the truth of the phrase, "money can't buy happiness."

Unfortunately, those who don't have lots of money continue to think that if they were to win the lottery or somehow gain a lot of money, it would reduce their problems. Yes, on one hand, it may reduce some problems, their immediate money related problems, but it will also create other problems that must be dealt with. Moreover, not all of one's problems are money related, and those will remain (i.e., dysfunctional family relationships, illness, personal or family health problems, death of a loved one, etc.). Therefore, money does not eliminate the problems or normal challenges of life. It just gives the wealthy some problems or challenges that are different from someone who is poor, but many of the problems or issues remain the same, namely, finding lasting happiness and peace, dealing with life in general, finding purpose and meaning in life, and relationship issues.

So, no one escapes the challenges of life that come from simply being alive in this world and striving to find lasting happiness. Yet, these challenges are very individualized. Many factors, including one's life experiences, influence one's perception as to which situation is a challenge or adversity and which one is not. What may be a challenging situation to one person may not be to others.

If The Stress Response Is A Good Thing, Why Do I Feel So Bad When I Become Stressed Out?

When you react to a non-life or death situation in a very emotional and fearful way and trigger the Stress Response, it's like calling a fire station and saying, *"please hurry, there is a REALLY bad fire going on here...it's a matter of life and death."* So the firepersons gear up, get their fire truck ready and rush over to your house, ready to fight the fire, and you come out and tell them, *"sorry guys, it was a false alarm."* Imagine all the energy they used up to get to your house...and there was no real fire.

Similarly, when the Stress Response is activated and the body gets all geared up for a life or death situation, and then the situation turns out not to be a life or death situation, a lot of energy is used up. This is why most people in our society feel tired, fatigued and stressed out a lot. It may be why you feel tired a lot. Not only are you burning up a lot of energy needlessly, but also the hormones and chemicals that are produced when the Stress Response is activated will still do the work they were summoned to do in the body, which is getting it ready to deal with a life or death situation. However, because there is no real life or death situation, the effects of the Stress

Response that would be helpful in a real life or death situation will now adversely affect your body, and also your mind and emotions, causing the signs and symptoms associated with stress.

In other words, if we trigger the Stress Response but we are not in a true life and death situation, then the effects of the Stress Response make us feel very bad emotionally, and can make us physically tired, weak, and even ill.

These bad feelings and effects of triggering the Stress Response (e.g., frustration, confusion, anger, anxiety, sadness, depression, etc,) for a false alarm are what people refer to as feeling *stressed out.* The signs of stress are discussed in more detail in the next section.

Emotional Signs of Stress (Being Stressed Out)

Cardiologist, Dr. Robert S. Eliot, in his book, *Is it worth Dying for?*, lists warning signs of stress[3]. Listed below are some signs of stress. These signs of stress are a result of reacting to situations that are not life or death situations, as if they were life or death situations, and therefore causing a false alarm activation of the Stress Response.

Some Early Warning Signs of Stress from *Is it worth Dying for?*:

- *Anger*
- *Irritability*
- *Inability to control violent impulses*
- *Defensive*
- *Arrogant*
- *Argumentative*
- *Rebellious*
- *Insecurity*
- *Sadness*
- *Feeling suspicious*
- *Preoccupied*
- *The "Blahs"*
- *Grandiosity (exaggerating the importance of your activities to yourself and others)"*

If you are having any of the above early signs of stress, it means you are triggering the Stress Response with false alarms, and you need to learn how to de-stress. You need to start practicing de-stressing techniques (will be covered later in this book).

De-stressing means learning how not to trigger the Stress Response with false alarms, how to stop the Stress Response if you accidentally trigger a false alarm, and how to recover from a false alarm activation of the Stress Response once it has run its course.

If so much stress builds up that a person cannot handle it and does not seek the proper help to deal with it, the mind can become overwhelmed, and the person can have a nervous breakdown. Sadly, some people even kill themselves (commit suicide) because of feeling so stressed out that they feel helpless[2]. Others turn to drugs, cigarettes (nicotine), alcohol or sex so as to not face how horrible and stressed out they feel.

Stress and Alcohol, Drugs, Cigarettes & Caffeine

Being dependent on drugs, cigarettes (nicotine), alcohol or sex are not good ways to handle stress, and to let stress control your life. They may temporarily mask the signs and symptoms of stress, but when their effects wear off, because the underlying reason for engaging in these behaviors, stress, was not properly handled, the symptoms of stress (anxiety, frustration, fear, etc.) will reemerge. At this point, there are three choices: 1) to implement effective de-stressing techniques, 2) continue to feel the discomfort of being stressed out, or 3) engage in the masking behavior again.

Some people choose to continue masking the signs and symptoms of stress. As a result, addictions develop. Because they did not take care of the underlying condition, stress, they feel compelled to engage in these behaviors over and over again, to keep masking the discomfort they

De-stressing = 1) Stop falsely triggering the Stress Response (SR). 2) Stop a falsely triggered SR. 3) Recuperate from a falsely triggered SR.

---

[2] 2004 National Institute of Mental Health Statistics: Suicide was the 11th leading cause of death in the U.S., and the third leading cause in children, adolescents and young adults (ages 10 – 24). World Health Organization: In 2000, one million people worldwide died from suicide.

are feeling due to stress; thus, the behavior eventually becomes a habit...an addiction.

If you must drink alcohol, including beer and wine, to be able to relax or have a good time at a party or other social gathering, or even when you are by yourself, you are stressed out and you need to take healthy measures to de-stress.

The same goes if you need to use tobacco products (cigarettes, etc.) or take other drugs to relax or have a good time. A person that is not stressed out will be able to relax and have a good time without drinking alcohol, smoking cigarettes or taking drugs. So, you can see that many people in our society are stressed out.

Drinking alcohol, especially beer and wine, smoking cigarettes, and doing drugs are very commonplace, so much so that they have become the normal thing to do at social events or in private...to be able to relax and or have a good time. They are compensatory coping activities that people have developed throughout history due to the incapacity to achieve natural relaxation. But these coping mechanisms are in fact dangerous to your health, and to the health of others around you (impaired judgment, alcohol or drug related accidents, second hand smoke, lung cancer, liver disease, etc.,).

In addition, drugs, cigarettes and alcohol actually promote the release of the stress hormones, which will intensify the negative effects of the falsely activated Stress Response. Therefore, instead of making you stress free, they actually make you more stressed out. According to cardiologist Dr Robert Eliot, nicotine can double to quadruple the amount of stress chemicals in your body[4].

Caffeine also exacerbates the Stress Response.

Don't let stress build up until you feel overwhelmed. It is important to know that if you are starting to feel really stressed out or already are so stressed out that you feel very sad, depressed, overwhelmed, unable to laugh or smile, helpless or that your life is out of control, you should seek help now. There are many qualified persons to help you learn to cope and de-stress.

Seeing a Psychologist or Psychiatrist

If you feel that you are not equipped to handle some situation in your life, or that your stress is pushing you and making you feel out of control in your life, it is time to get some help. Psychologists are professionals who work with people and teach them how to cope with life and de-stress; they are also called therapists. If your condition is more serious and the therapist feels you would benefit from medication, the therapist may refer you to a psychiatrist. A psychiatrist is a medical doctor who specializes in treating conditions affecting the mind and emotions, including stress. Therapists and psychiatrists can assist you with parenting, relationship, work, grief, illness and other issues; they can provide you with effective tools to deal with your specific situation. In addition, they will likely teach you some relaxation techniques to start you on the road to de-stressing.

> Ask for help if you feel over-whelmed or out of control. It shows a lot of maturity to be able to ask for help when you need it.

It shows a lot of maturity to be able to ask for help when you need it. We all need help from others at some time in life. Sometimes people are afraid to go to a psychologist or psychiatrist because they think other people will think they are crazy, but real craziness is allowing stress to make you unhappy and stressed out.

Taking Medications For Stress

Sometimes people may need to take certain prescription medication(s) for a period of time to help them relax, until they learn to apply the tools of coping and de-stressing, at which time, they can usually discontinue the medication(s). Medications can have serious side effects, so they should only be taken if a qualified health care practitioner that treats stress recommends doing so. Also, because different health care practitioners may treat extreme stress slightly differently, you may wish to get a second opinion before taking medication, or concerning when to stop taking it.

Note to Youth and Children:

If you are a child or youth, talk to your parents and or other adults in your life and tell them you need help to deal with your stress.

Do not give up if some adults do not seem to understand how badly you are feeling, or are unable to help you. Most parents and other adults do not know how to effectively de-stress. Your parents may have never learnt it, which is why they did not teach it to you, or maybe they only know a little about it.

If your parents cannot seem to help you, tell them you want to go to a psychologist. Also, most schools usually have a school psychologist. No one but you and your parent(s) have to know that you are going to a psychologist.

Psychologists have to keep whatever you tell them confidential, that is, between you and them, and depending on how old you are, or what the circumstances are, they may also meet and talk with your parent(s) or guardian so your parent(s) or guardian can better understand what you are going through and know how to best help you.

In addition, don't feel bad if your parents have to help you with this.

You will actually be helping them by them learning to help you, because they will also be learning how to de-stress themselves and become healthier and happier.

Physical Effects Of Being Stressed Out

In addition to the effects on the mind and emotions, the false alarm activation of the Stress Response that we call undue stress or being stressed out also affects the physical body. The following are signs or symptoms that you may experience because of a false alarm activation of the Stress Response:

- headaches, migraines
- back problems
- acid indigestion, upset stomach
- stomach or intestinal cramps
- nausea
- diarrhea
- vomiting
- weak immune system
- low energy, fatigue
- angina

And over a long period of time, the false alarm activation of the Stress Response can cause or be associated with some serious health problems, including:

- heart disease, heart attacks
- diabetes
- stomach ulcers
- high blood pressure, which can cause stroke and kidney disease
- high cholesterol
- immune problems
- cancer

So, if you have any of these conditions, they may be stress-related, and in addition to seeking medical attention to take care of the physical problems, you also need to learn how to de-stress.

Seeking medical help for the symptoms one may be experiencing related to stress can be frustrating, because especially in the early stages of stress where the long term complications of chronic stress have not yet manifested in disease, the diagnostic tests that doctors run often come back negative.

So, even though you are experiencing lots of discomfort, doctors may tell you that they cannot find anything physically wrong with you. They may give you medications to palliate the symptoms you are experiencing, such as antacids to relieve your acid reflux, etc., and you may experience some relief.

However, realize that if you do not take measures to reduce or eliminate the underlying cause of the symptoms, stress, the condition is not likely to go away, and may in fact worsen; also, the symptoms may persist or worsen in spite of the medication(s). Therefore, you must also implement de-stressing techniques to reduce or eliminate the source of the problem, false activation of the Stress Response (stress).

Chapter 2: You Have The Power

Defining Stress

Remember the definition I gave of being stressed out above:

The bad feelings and effects we feel when we trigger the Stress Response for a false alarm.

Other people give stress different definitions, but some of these definitions can be misleading, and more importantly, they do not give us power over our lives, but rather, give situations in our lives the power to keep triggering the Stress Response and keep us stressed out.

For example, the American Heritage Dictionary gives the following definitions of stress:

1) A mentally or emotionally disruptive or upsetting condition occurring in response to adverse external influences and capable of affecting physical health, usually characterized by increased heart rate, a rise in blood pressure, muscular tension, irritability, and depression.

2) A stimulus or circumstance causing such a condition.

3) A state of extreme difficulty, pressure, or strain.

The first definition says stress is when we become emotionally or mentally upset because of some unfavorable situation that is occurring in our life, and it causes physical changes in our body that can affect our physical health and be associated with emotional disturbances as well (irritability and depression). It is great that this definition discusses that stress affects our physical and mental-emotional health, because until recently, many doctors did not recognize this. However, science has also shown that people become stressed out not only in adverse conditions, but also in circumstances that should be joyous, such as preparing for a wedding or winning a lottery. Definition #2 says that stress is the event or circumstance that causes us to become emotionally or mentally upset and trigger the Stress Response to cause the physical symptoms of stress. And definition #3 says when we feel stressed, we are in a state of extreme difficulty, pressure or strain.

One problem with definitions #1 and #2 above is they link stress (being stressed out) to factors outside of ourselves, factors that we have no control over ("...in response to adverse external influences..."; "a stimulus or circumstance causing such a condition"). We can try to exert our control over others or our environment, but really, we ultimately cannot, because everyone else is trying to do the same, and their opinion of what is good often does not agree with ours. So, the only thing we can really control is us; we can learn to control our feelings and responses to difficult situations. This is important to know, because this is where the power to de-stress comes from.

> You can control how you respond to a situation.

You may not have control over what is going on in the world, if you get a flat tire or not, if it rains or not, if your boss or teacher is having a bad day or not, but you can become proficient in learning to react to these and other challenging situations of life without becoming stressed out. In other words, you can control you...your thoughts, the emotions/feelings they generate, and your reaction to the situation. Then it does not matter what non-life or death situation life brings your way; you will be able to remain calm and handle it without becoming stressed out.

Another problem with definitions #1 and #2, and also definition #3, is that they don't differentiate between situations that are life or death versus situations that are difficult, a strain, cause you to feel pressurized, but are NOT a matter of life or death. In other words, they do not distinguish between feeling stressed out (false activation of the Stress Response) and the appropriate activation of the Stress Response (a life or death situation).

Stressed Out = reacting to a NON-life or death situation as if it were a life or death situation.

The Stress Response is a normal physiologic response to a life or death situation. Being stressed out is reacting to a non-life or death situation (non-life-threatening situation), as if it were a life or death situation. This means that in the latter situation, stress is occurring because of a thought process that is incorrect...that is not real...because there is no real life or death situation occurring, just as in the example above with the firepersons gearing up for a fire that turns out to be a false alarm. Therefore, it is an incorrect way of thinking and feeling about and reacting to a non-life or death situation that causes one to become stressed out.

Stressed Out = a wrongful way of thinking.

If your situation it is not life-threatening, you don't need the SR and you don't need to feel stressed out.

The situation may be difficult, challenging, painful, hurtful, a blow to your ego, embarrassing, nerve-racking, or unfair, but if it is NOT a life or death situation, you don't need your Stress Response, and therefore, you don't need to feel stressed out, the effects of triggering the Stress Response as a false alarm.

So, it is important to realize that stress is not about a particular situation (i.e., the external circumstance) in which you find yourself, but how you respond to a situation that is not a matter of life or death: *Are you responding to it as if it were a life or death situation?* If you are, then you will feel stressed out. However, if you do not respond to it as if it were a life or death situation, you will not feel stressed out. This is an important point to understand, because this is what gives you control over your stress. Your level of stress is directly proportional to the emotional intensity with which you react to non-life or death situations rather than to the situations themselves. Understanding this will allow you to take control over if you become stressed out or not. Understanding this means understanding that you have the potential to control if you become stressed out or not in any situation, because it is possible for you to control the emotional intensity with which you respond to non-life or death situations. However, if you believe that your stress level is due to the external circumstances in your life over which you have minimal or no control, then you will feel powerless and susceptible to stress.

> With practice, you can control the intensity of emotion with which you respond to a situation, and thus control and reduce your level of stress.

There is always something affecting our lives about which we can choose to become upset. We could become upset and stressed out about the fact it is raining and we can't go to the beach like we planned. We could become upset that someone scratched our car. We could become upset that our teacher or boss yelled at us because they were all stressed out and reacted as if they were in a life or death situation. If stress were caused by situations in our lives, then we would have NO control, because life is nothing but different, changing situations…many of which challenge us in some way.

Also, if the cause of stress were the situation, then everybody should find the same situations to be equally stressful, and react the same to them, but this is not the case. Different people react differently to the same situation. Some people become stressed out by a teacher or boss treating them unfairly, while others do not. Some people become stressed out when someone disagrees with them, while others do not. Some people become stressed out when traffic is backed up, while others do not. Some people become stressed out when their car gets a flat tire in a parking lot, while others do not.

So, it is not the situation that holds the key to feeling stressed out, but how you handle and react to the situation. Do you get so upset that you send messages telling your mind and body that you are in a life or death situation, and to activate the Stress Response?

Fortunately, feeling stressed out is not ultimately caused by situations in your life, nor is it ultimately controlled by those situations either. It is not your boss or teacher treating you badly, or the test you have to take, or your parent(s) grounding you, or being late for school and getting detention, or getting fired from your job, or having someone yell or curse at you, etc., that makes you feel stressed out.

Great news: You can control and eliminate stress.

What causes you to feel stressed out in these situations is becoming very upset or afraid and reacting to these circumstances as if they were life or death, when they are not. THIS IS GREAT NEWS!!! It is great news because it means YOU CAN CONTROL AND ELIMINATE STRESS from your life!!! You have the power to control how you feel and act.

Now granted, for some people this may be easier said than done, because although every person has the capacity to have control over how they feel and how they act, not everyone has worked to develop this capacity within themselves. If overreacting to non-life or death situations with a lot of anger or fear has become a habit, and from the detrimental effects it causes, mentally-emotionally and physically, we can say it is a bad habit, then it will take time to break this bad habit and develop a new, good habit of not overreacting.

Two important aspects of de-stressing are learning how to not trigger the Stress Response as a false alarm, and how to stop the false alarm triggering of the Stress Response once it has been activated.

Even when successfully practicing the de-stressing techniques, you may still feel hurt, embarrassed, treated unfairly, challenged, etc., in difficult situations, but you will not feel all stressed out. In other words, you will not feel that *"this is a big crisis, and it's going to kill me"*; rather, you will handle it and get through it without making yourself sick and upset.

Being stressed out means that at some level you are feeling that a non-life-threatening situation in your life is not only a threat to your general well-being, but to your very life. However, because the situation is non-life-threatening, this perception is not true. Rather, it is the overreacting to the situation as if it were a life or death situation that can kill you...you can have a heart attack, stroke, etc. And this is what inappropriate stress is...overreacting to a non-life or death situation with such intense emotions that your mind-body complex develops the idea that you must be in a life or death crisis, and therefore sets out to save your life...by activating the Stress Response.

So if you do not become all stressed out, that is, react to a situation with such overwhelming emotion that you falsely trigger the activation of the natural Stress Response that should be reserved for crisis situations, you will not risk killing yourself right there and then by having a heart attack or stroke. You also will not be exposing yourself to all those bad feelings and signs of stress...i.e., feeling stressed out.

You will be able to put the situation into a more realistic perspective:

> *Well, this is unfair, but thank goodness, it is not a matter of life or death. Well, this is embarrassing...but thank goodness, it is not a matter of life or death. I feel really hurt by this situation, but thank goodness it's not a matter of life or death. My financial situation is a bit scary right now...I am not sure what I am going to do, but thank goodness it is not a matter of life or death. I lost my job and do not know how I will pay my mortgage/rent...I do not know how the situation will work itself out, but thank goodness it is not a matter of life or death.*

If the Stress Response is not triggered as a false alarm, the emotions you are experiencing will not bother you as much because they will not be worsened or intensified by all the negative physical effects and feelings that would be affecting you if the Stress Response were unnecessarily triggered. The negative emotions are associated with the effects of the falsely triggered Stress Response. So, if you don't trigger it, you won't get all stressed out, and you will find that you will actually be able to think clearly in the situation and deal with it from a point of inner strength and calmness; you are less likely to say something you will regret or act impulsively and do something you would regret. Therefore, you have a better capacity to handle the situation.

You can handle a difficult situation more effectively when you are not stressed out.

What will happen if you do not allow yourself to get so upset and overwhelmed by non-life-threatening situations to the extent that you falsely activate the Stress Response?

Well, most significantly, you will be eliminating the risk of triggering a real life or death situation for yourself, such as having a heart attack[5] or stroke (from falsely activating the Stress Response). Secondly, you will be eliminating the bad feelings and signs of stress.

You may still be facing very difficult circumstances and choices in your life situation. No doubt, some of life's predicaments can be very serious and you may not like the options you have to choose between...especially if you feel that your choice is between the lesser of two evils. However, consider this point: *When has reacting in a very upset manner ever solved your past problems?* It may have appeared to have provided some catharsis and allowed you to let off steam, but the negative physiologic effects still occurred, and at some point you still had to get down to the business of dealing with the situation, which boils down to working to change/improve the situation and accepting what you cannot change about the situation.

Getting Stressed Out and Letting off Steam...Is it worth it?

Let's look at the *"getting upset to let off steam"* way of reacting to situations. Consider that the steam you are letting off is your energy...energy that you are burning up and won't have to put towards solving the problem at hand. Also consider the health risks: heart attack, stroke, hypertension (high blood pressure), high cholesterol, feeling sad, feeling depressed, feeling anxious, worrying a lot, etc. So, ask yourself if the cathartic effect from letting off steam is worth dying for? Or worth becoming paralyzed for (i.e., if you have a stroke)? Or worth getting ulcers for? Or worth becoming sick over? Or worth having a nervous breakdown over? Or worth feeling bad over? Dr. Robert S. Eliot, author of the book, *Is It Worth Dying For?*, concluded NO!, after he, a cardiologist, had a heart attack, triggered by stress. What's your answer? Is it worth it? Don't skip over answering this question. If your answer is not a firm NO!...it's NOT worth it, then you are not ready to de-stress.

If you feel your situation is so much different than everyone else's, that if the best stress management teacher were in your shoes, they too would be totally stressed out, you may be right. Maybe your life is out of control. If this is your situation, pay extra attention when you read Chapter 3 below, *Meeting The Basic Needs*; you may even want to skip ahead and read this section first. However, if your life is not out of control, and yet you feel that your situation is more difficult than a lot of other people's situations, maybe it is. But, the point still remains that if your situation is not one of life or death, then you don't need to trigger your Stress Response and feel stressed out. Consider that there are people who face real life or death situations with a cool and calm disposition. You must clearly understand that it is NOT the situation that causes you to feel stressed out, but YOUR overreaction to the situation, and therefore, you should seek to de-stress.

Getting Stressed Out by Good News

The Stress Response is not only activated in situations you perceive to be adverse in some way. There are documented instances of people winning the lottery and dying of a heart attack shortly after being given the "great" news. They were emotionally overwhelmed by the situation. They overreacted to the news. The extreme emotional overreaction set off a false alarm activation of the Stress Response. Reacting as if winning the lottery was going to "save their life" made the winning of the lottery a matter of life or death, and therefore falsely triggered the Stress Response. The truth is that winning the lottery for most people is not literally a matter of life or death.

Winning the lottery might allow you to live a monetarily wealthier life, but not necessarily a better quality of life, and even the former is questionable, as research shows that a substantial number of lottery winners lose their winnings within five years. So, emotional extremes are to be avoided, as extreme overreaction, regardless of if you perceive the situation to be negative or positive, can cause a false alarm triggering of the Stress Response.

Persevere with Patience – Change is Usually a Gradual Process

Do not expect that you will go from being someone who is always letting off steam or overreacting in circumstances you find difficult or unfair, etc., to being as cool as a cucumber, metaphorically speaking, overnight. It is possible for such a profound change to occur in your personality in a short time if you really "get it," that is, if you really understand that you can choose ***not to*** react to life's situations that are not a matter of life or death as if they were a matter of life or death, no matter how difficult you may feel the situation is, and if there is already an established basis in your unconscious mind for eliminating the habit of overreacting.

However, for most people, the change will be gradual and building. In other words, you may continue to overreact, but the intensity of the episodes and length of time they last will lessen as you continue to apply the tools of de-stressing. This is a VERY important point, because although you may still find yourself continuing to overreact and getting all stressed out in certain situations, don't feel that you did not "get it," that is, that you do not understand that stress is detrimental to you, and that you can control it. Rather understand the process of change, that it takes time, and allow the process to unfold, with patience, as you persevere in de-stressing.

Be patient with yourself. Change is a gradual process.

Therefore, do not judge your success in de-stressing in an all or nothing manner, *"I am still getting stressed out so this de-stressing stuff is not working."*

Judge your success in de-stressing by noting if the intensity and frequency of stressed out episodes have decreased as compared to the previous week, month or year, rather than if they still occur.

Rather, evaluate success by noting if, with each passing week, month, or year, the number of times you feel all stressed out is decreasing. Suppose you use to feel stressed out several times a day, and now you only feel stressed out once a day…that is progress! You are becoming more stress-free. Suppose you used to feel stressed out everyday, and now you only feel stressed out every other day…that is progress! Suppose previously it would have taken you three days to calm down from a stressful episode, but now by applying the de-stressing tools, you are able to calm down in two days…that is progress! If you continue to apply the de-stressing tools, the frequency and intensity of the stress attacks and the length of time it takes you to recuperate will continue to decrease…until the habit is broken.

Furthermore, use the opportunity provided by any situation you find to be challenging to intensify your practice of the de-stressing techniques.

Every time you notice that you are in the "all stressed out" mode, choose one or more of the de-stressing tools that would be most suited to your circumstance and environment (i.e., where you are, work or school versus home, alone versus in a crowd of people, etc.) and put it/them into action right away: practice, practice, practice. Remember the adage: *practice makes perfect.*

Stress and Chronic Life Threatening Illness of Oneself or a Family Member

If you have a life-threatening illness, then the activation of the Stress Response may be appropriate, depending on your circumstances. However, if you are not in an immediate life or death crisis, you are also likely experiencing stress due to false activation of the Stress Response. Illness in general can evoke stress, because of the possibility that one's condition may worsen and become life threatening; therefore, people with serious illnesses are often very stressed out. Even so, while you are alive and are not in an immediate crisis, you can derive benefit from many of the de-stressing tools, especially because as was discussed above, stress is associated with many conditions of ill health. Many hospitals even offer classes on various de-stressing techniques for patients. You should consult your doctor to discuss which de-stressing tools would be appropriate for you before starting a de-stressing program. You should also seek counseling with a therapist as well. Many patients benefit emotionally as well as with respect to their physical health from counseling, including group counseling and support groups.

> De-stressing is important if you are ill, because being ill can cause one to feel stressed out, and this stress could worsen the illness.

If you are a caregiver for someone who is critically ill, it is a difficult situation. But for you, it is not a matter of your life or death, so your Stress Response is generally not needed, except if you have to act to save the person's life in a crisis. If you are feeling the effects of stress or burnout[3], you should practice de-stressing on a regular basis, including speaking to a therapist as well. You will also derive benefit from a support group.

---

[3] "This pandemic, looming large and threatening health care as a whole, is the burn-out syndrome striking those providing care for people with chronic illness…" Sartorius N., **An epidemic is threatening health care worldwide.** Croat Med J. 2005 Feb;46(1):152-3.

Chapter 3: Meeting the Basic Needs (Nutrition and Rest)

Unsustainable Lifestyle activation of the Stress Response:

If at this point in reading this book, you feel that you cannot benefit from this book because you are not stressed out from overreacting to situations, but because your life is very stressful, you may be correct. It very well may be that your life situation itself is the source of the feelings and signs you are attributing to stress. However, you are not feeling that way because you are stressed out (false activation of the Stress Response), but rather, you are feeling the actual effects of an appropriate activation of the Stress Response because of the way you are living life. In other words, your lifestyle is the problem.

The physical body has certain basic needs that must be met to sustain it and keep it alive. For example, a person who is deprived of sleep will eventually die[4]. A person who is deprived of food (proper nutrients) or water will become progressively weaker and die. So, food (proper nutrients), water, clean air, and on average 8 – 10 hours of sleep[5] are basic necessities of the physical body...for its survival. There are others, but these are the major ones.

If the physical body is not given the bare minimum of any or all of these necessities, or given just enough for it to survive, the Stress Response is going to be activated all the time. Just like a car left with the engine running all the time

---

[4] Sleep is a vital nutrient for the mind-body complex. Consider that a person can survive longer without food than without sleep.

[5] Some people may require less sleep; the amount of sleep a person needs depends on several factors, including age of the person (elderly people need less sleep generally), one's activity level, one's level of stress, if one engages in de-stressing techniques on a regular basis, as well as other lifestyle factors.

will eventually overheat and malfunction, the ongoing Stress Response will also create conditions of malfunction for the body, and predispose it to the same conditions of ill-health (mental-emotional and physical) that stress due to false alarm activation of the Stress Response causes, including death. Therefore, these necessities must be met at some level above the basic requirements for survival.

The mind[6] also has needs as well, the most basic one being the need to rest. Sleep provides this, but sleep is not totally restful for the mind, because the mind is still working, though not on a conscious level, when one dreams (REM {rapid eye movement} sleep). In addition, as you have most likely experienced, worries and anxieties can work their way into dreams and not only cause nightmares that can activate the Stress Response during sleep, but also restlessness and insomnia. Dreams can also serve the individual in a beneficial way, such as assisting the individual in resolving certain mental complexes or bringing forth inspirational messages or experiences. But dreams can also prevent both the mind and body from getting a good night's rest. It is only during deep sleep (non-REM, non-dream) that the mind is able to really rest during sleep. Therefore, depending on how many dreams one has, one's mind may or may not get much rest during sleep.

[6] When I use the term mind, I am not referring to the brain or nervous system, unless specifically stated. The brain and Nervous System are being categorized with the physical body. The term "mind" is being used here to refer to the subtle thought processes (conscious, subconscious, unconscious) that is linked to the emotions and intellect.

The mind's need for rest is even greater in the modern technological age where the preponderance of work is mental rather than physical, as in the past. So, the modern Western lifestyle generally tasks the mind more than the physical body. Thus, generally speaking, in our modern technology-oriented culture, while the mind needs more rest, the physical body needs more exercise.

Sleep is one way to rest the mind, but there are other ways to rest it in the awake state. Most people only rest their minds when they sleep, because they find it impossible to sit still and not think of their problems. So, what they seek to do instead if they want to stop worrying about certain situations and stay awake at the same time is to distract the mind from the unwanted thoughts. In the West, the most popular pastime for distracting the mind is watching television. While it serves to distract the mind from its preoccupations, it is still agitating the mind, and making it think and jump about from one thought to the next, as do most of the other alternatives people use to distract themselves from the nagging thoughts. Moreover, the minute the television is turned off or other distracting activity ends, the mind goes back to its worries.

Eating is also another activity that people commonly use to distract themselves from their worries, and often eating junk food; this can lead to overeating, weight gain and obesity.

So, distraction is a limited and generally ineffective way to rest the mind. The Deep Breathing Concentration Technique given in *Chapter 9* below is a more effective means of resting the mind while in the awake state.

When the basic needs of the body and mind are not met, the survival of the person is threatened, and thus, the Stress Response is triggered. Therefore, if one's life situation is such that it does not allow the basic needs of the body and mind to be met, i.e., food (proper nutrition), rest, water (many people do not drink enough water daily and become chronically dehydrated), etc., one is in fact putting one's life at risk by internally creating a life or death, life-threatening, situation from ongoing activation of the Stress Response. This is even more ironic when people are caught up in such a lifestyle...to survive. In other words, they are risking death (by creating an actual life-threatening situation), because they want to live.

If someone is living in such circumstances because they are impoverished or live in a region of the world plagued by famine, drought, war or pestilence, etc., and have no other options for survival, then the activation of the Stress Response, though detrimental on a long-term basis, is appropriate; these really are life or death situations. Therefore, what I am speaking about here is an artificially created life or death situation, where the person has other options they could exercise to live life in a non-life or death manner (a way that does not activate the Stress Response on an ongoing basis), but for whatever reasons they choose not to do so.

Self-created lifestyle activation of the Stress Response

Self-created lifestyle activation of the Stress Response, which can feel exactly like being stressed out, is when one lives in an environment where one has the capacity to sustain the basic needs of one's body and mind, but yet one deprives oneself of these basic needs and puts the body at risk of dying, i.e., such as by having a heart attack or stroke...in other words, one creates a life threatening situation.

One may be working too much and not getting enough sleep[7]. Thus, the body and mind are not getting the basic needs of rest met.

One may be working too much and skipping meals and or not eating nutritiously. Thus, the body is not getting the basic need of food/nutrition met, which weakens it and

---

[7] Benson H. Are you working too hard? A conversation with mind/body researcher Herbert Benson. Harv Bus Rev. 2005 Nov;83(11):53-8, 165: "In total, American businesses lose $300 billion annually to lowered productivity, absenteeism, health-care, and related costs stemming from stress."

makes it susceptible to numerous conditions of ill health, some of which can occur right away (i.e., dizziness, fatigue etc.), or later on in life (immune conditions, cancer, etc.).

One may be living in a polluted environment, smoking, or not breathing properly (discussed in Chapter 8, #3). Thus, the body may not be getting enough clean air to meet its basic needs.

Situations where the body-mind complex is deprived of its basic needs are often compounded by addiction to substances that further activate the Stress Response and damage the body in other ways, such as alcohol, which kills liver cells in addition to activating the Stress Response, and cigarettes, which fill the body, especially the lungs, with poisons such as carbon monoxide, in addition to activating the Stress Response.

So, it is the person's overall lifestyle that is triggering the Stress Response. In this case, however, the triggering of the Stress Response is quite appropriate. What is not appropriate is the complexity of life that many people have created for themselves. They have created lifestyles that are incompatible with living a healthy life...literally a time bomb waiting to explode, by their having a heart attack, stroke, or other complications that can arise from the ongoing and long-term triggering of the Stress Response, which are the same signs and illnesses caused by stress due to false activation of the Stress Response.

> Many people have created lifestyles that are incompat -ible with living a healthy life.

This scenario is very common in the West, especially the USA. It happens when greater priority is given to fulfilling desires that are not related to one's survival than to meeting the basic survival needs of the body-mind complex. People may not even realize that they have made this choice in their lives. To them, they are just living life, and they don't understand how or why they feel so stressed out. They may blame their jobs, their bosses, their family, their spouses, etc. But they never sit down to take a good look at how they are living, and understand that they have created a lifestyle that is stressful based on their need to fulfill certain desires...a lifestyle that is always a matter of life or death, and that can eventually become incompatible with life. Sometimes it takes their surviving a heart attack or some other serious illness to start thinking about how they are living their lives, and seek an alternative way of living life.

Thus, Westerners have found a way to create a situation whereby their very lifestyle becomes a matter of life or death, by choice, although that choice may have been made unconsciously by trying to fulfill various desires for status, emotional support, etc. People living like this often say they need to de-stress, or they want to learn de-stressing techniques, but they never make any effort to do so beyond saying they want to, because they really don't have the time and or energy to partake in such activities. If they did have the time, they would use it to eat properly and or get proper rest; they would use it to meet the basic needs of their body-mind complex.

So, this is something you need to evaluate, because if your lifestyle does not permit you to meet the basic needs of your body and mind, then applying the tools of de-stressing is not the foremost answer, because you really are in a life or death situation. Therefore, first and foremost, you need to take measures to end the life threatening way in which you are living your life. You need to focus on meeting the basic needs of your body-mind complex to stop the frequent or almost continuous activation of the Stress Response. De-stressing can assist you during the process of making the transition, and also afterwards to recuperate and bring your body-mind complex back into balance. I want to emphasize however, that de-stressing will be limited in its effectiveness if the main situation of meeting the basic needs of the body-mind complex are not met.

Socioeconomic Stress Response Activation

The cost of living has increased over the years, and salaries have not always matched cost of living increases. In addition, in many areas, property taxes and cost of purchasing a home have dramatically increased, so that persons wishing to remain in a certain community may not be able to do so unless they work two jobs, or make other sacrifices. Then add to this the normal difficulties and challenges of life that you do not have control over, such as illness of a family member, accidents, natural events (storms, hurricanes, tornadoes, floods), etc.

If this is your situation, and you are stressed out because you are unable to meet your basic body-mind requirements for a healthy life, then you need to look for alternatives. You may need to move in with a family member if that is possible so as to share expenses, or if this is not possible, you may need to move to another location (town, city, state, country) where the cost of living is cheaper, and you can work a reasonable amount of hours and make enough money to sustain your basic needs. You may have to make sacrifices, such as moving away from family or friends, but you will no doubt make new friends, and you may even have enough money left over after taking care of your basic needs to take trips to visit your family, and equally, they can visit you. They may even decide to move near you to also enjoy a slower paced – less stress lifestyle.

The bottom line is that if your present circumstances are a constant life or death struggle at the most basic level of meeting the needs of the physical body and mind, and you don't do something to improve your circumstances, you could die...in this life or death struggle. So, ask yourself, is whatever that is keeping you locked in this struggle, fear of the unknown, fear of moving away from family and or friends, etc., worth the risk of dying over? Your friends or family would not want you to kill yourself to be near them. Perhaps, like you, they do not realize that you are in a constant life or death struggle.

If you suspect or recognize this is your situation, but cannot face or confront the emotional issues that are preventing you from moving forward to improve your situation, seek counseling from a qualified therapist/psychologist.

You may also consider contacting a financial counselor and job/career counselor to see if there are other options that you may not have considered, which may allow you to be able to work less and meet your basic needs where you currently live. You should also meet with a realtor to see if there is a cheaper housing option in your area or surrounding areas, even if it requires a short commute.

Until you get yourself out of this situation, you will find it difficult, if not impossible, to effectively de-stress. First of all, if you don't have time to sleep or eat properly, you likely won't have any or much time to practice the de-stressing tools. Also, even if you do practice de-stressing, your Stress Response motor is always running, because your situation is one of constant struggle, a constant battle of life or death, and this will also minimize the effectiveness of these techniques.

However, if you are able to apply any of the de-stressing tools, the benefit you derive may allow you to keep your head above water, so to speak, while you work to improve your living situation to make your life a sustainable one. However, you still need to make changes to improve your life situation. The important point is to realize that this is your situation; then you can understand why you are feeling stressed, and begin to make adjustments and seek positive and healthy alternatives to your current situation.

Stress Response Activation Due to Too Many Desires

Many people earning good salaries, living in nice houses and driving nice cars are stressed out. This is especially common in the West. Many people who live with their Stress Response in a continuous or almost continuous state of activation due to their life situation being incompatible with sustaining the basic needs of their body and mind are in the socioeconomic middle or upper class. This is because in spite of earning enough to sustain the basic needs of their mind and body, they spend in excess of what they earn because they have lots of desires and very little will power or self-control, or want to be regarded with a higher status by their peers or those they wish to impress in their community.

Perhaps they want the status of living in a certain neighborhood, or the status of driving a certain type of car/vehicle, or the status of their children attending a certain school, having a boat, etc.

The result is that even though they earn a good living that could provide all their basic necessities for a sustainable life, they live as if they are socioeconomically impaired (poor). And rather than choosing to downscale their lives and desires and make adjustments so that they can work an appropriate work day (no more than 6-8 hours) and an appropriate work week (no more than 30-40 hours), or be able to stay home with their young child(ren) and comfortably support themselves, taking care of meeting their basic needs as well as putting away savings...they choose the option of working more hours to make more money to support an upscale lifestyle.

If this is your situation, you need to reconsider your priorities, and realize that you are putting your life at risk. You need to make whatever adjustments are necessary to allow you to sustain the basic needs of your physical body and mind.

You should consult experts in various areas to decide on how best to proceed. You may need to begin by speaking to a psychologist or therapist to work through the emotional reason(s) that have created such a strong desire to live above your financial means and learn how to let it/them go. In addition, as discussed in the above section, *Socioeconomic Stress Response Activation,* you may also wish to contact a financial planner and realtor to discuss your options.

Until you make the needed adjustments in your life, de-stressing will be of limited benefit to you for the same reasons given in the section above, *Socioeconomic Stress Response Activation.*

However, as stated above, if you have the time and can practice some of the de-stressing tools, the benefit you derive may allow you to keep your head above water, so to speak, while you work to improve your living situation to make your life a sustainable one.

Part 2: Understanding Stress and The Relationship Between Health, Diet and Stress

Chapter 4: Physiology of Stress

Before we proceed to learn the specific techniques for de-stressing, first you need to understand the Stress Response in depth, how it works, and how it causes the physical effects we experience in a true life or death emergency or in a state of being stressed out. This way you will be able to observe yourself to recognize the onset of the physical signs caused by the activation of the Stress Response to know when you are becoming stressed out.

In addition, understanding the workings of the Stress Response will allow you to relate the physical effects that result from the activation of the Stress Response to specific conditions of ill health. The information in this chapter will also lay a foundation for your understanding of the relationship between stress, diet and ill health that will be discussed in detail in the next two chapters. Further, it will allow you to see how and why the tools for de-stressing that are presented in this book work to prevent the Stress Response from being triggered, break the Stress Response once it has been triggered, or allow you to recuperate from the effects of a falsely activated Stress Response.

How the Stress Response Works

The Stress Response is mediated by a part of your Nervous System called the Sympathetic Nervous System. The Sympathetic Nervous System (SNS) has an opposite counterpart, the Parasympathetic Nervous System (PSNS). Therefore, the PSNS is our key to preventing, stopping and recuperating from the Stress Response. So we will learn about it as well.

It is important to understand that although the SNS is associated with activation of the Stress Response, the SNS is not our enemy. The Nervous System is set up so that the SNS and PSNS interact with each other in a way that balances the functions of the body. We need our SNS to function normally and be healthy; it mobilizes us into action. We also need our PSNS; it allows us to be calm and restful. In addition, these two systems interact with each other in many other very specific ways to keep our bodies functioning normally.

The problem arises when we overuse the SNS, either by living life in an extreme manner (unsustainable lifestyle as discussed in Chapter 3 above) or by reacting to life in a stressed out manner. Then the SNS is pushed out of balance by overuse, and the PSNS is also pushed out of balanced by under use (it is suppressed). Therefore, efforts must be made to bring the body back to a balance by normalizing these two systems, which means decreasing the activity of the SNS and increasing the activity of the PSNS; this is how the de-stressing tools work.

> De-stressing tools work by bringing the body back into balance.

SNS Geared for Life or Death Situation

The body undergoes many changes when the Stress Response is activated by the SNS. These responses are all geared towards maximizing your survival in a life or death situation. The basic way this works in a life or death situation is:

1. A part of the brain triggers nerve impulses and releases hormones.

2. The hormones stimulate the adrenal glands, which are two small glands that are located near the kidneys.

3. When the adrenal glands are stimulated, they release two chemical compounds into the bloodstream: adrenaline & cortisol.

4. These chemicals (adrenaline & cortisol) as well as the nerves that are stimulated have several effects on the physical body, all of them designed to increase one's survival in a life or death situation:

   o They make the heart beat faster and harder to pump more blood to the muscles to give them more oxygen for energy so they have energy to run away (flight response) or fight off the danger (fight response).

   o They cause the breathing to become more rapid in an attempt to increase the oxygen getting to the lungs and then into the blood stream to provide the fuel for energy for the body; the breath also becomes shallower as a result of the rapid breathing.

   o They cause the blood vessels that take blood from the heart (arteries) to decrease in size (constrict), which causes the blood pressure to increase, just as if you kept the same amount of water flowing through a hose but squeezed it to make the diameter narrower, the pressure of the water would increase and it would come out with more force. So, this also causes the blood to move faster through the body, transporting oxygen to the tissues and carrying away the waste products that are being built up from the increased energy usage.

o They categorize the body's systems into two parts: 1) vital systems that need blood and oxygen to be able to fight or take flight, and 2) non-vital systems that are not so essential to survival in the immediate future and can be temporarily shut down.

So, blood to organs like the stomach and intestines (gastro-intestinal system) and kidneys are diverted to other systems that need it more in this time of crisis, like the muscles. The appetite is turned off. After all, if something were trying to kill you, it would not be a good thing for you to get hungry and want to stop to eat. Also, when you are in a struggle for life or death, you don't want to have to stop to urinate, so little urine is produced since the kidneys are not receiving much blood.

o They decrease blood flow to the skin, hands and feet (resulting in cold hands and cold feet, which are also signs of stress), so that if there is an injury, there will be less loss of blood.

o They cause the release of fats, including cholesterol, into the blood stream; these fats are used for energy.

o They cause an increase in glucose (blood sugar) to provide energy.

o They cause the blood to clot faster; in case of injury the person would be less likely to bleed to death.

- o They cause the eyes to open wide and the pupils of the eyes to dilate so you can get a broader view of what is around you.

- o They cause you to sweat so that the sweat can cool off the body as it is either fighting or running, to prevent overheating.

- o They cause the stomach to secrete more acid so that if there is an injury, the extra acid will kill off bacteria and prevent infection.

- o They cause an immediate evacuation of the urinary bladder and bowels to lighten the body's load to make it easier to flee, or to reduce the risk of injury to those tissues and contamination of the abdomen with their contents in case of injury if one stays to fight.

So, as you can see, all of these changes caused by the Stress Response are quite important for survival in a life or death situation. If you are in a life or death emergency, you want your heart to beat faster to circulate more blood to the vital organs and tissues, your blood pressure to increase, your stomach to produce more acid, your body to sweat, a lot of cholesterol, fats and glucose in your bloodstream to be used for energy, your blood to clot faster, your appetite to be shut off, etc. But if it is not a life or death situation, then these changes unnecessarily cause the physical and emotional signs and symptoms of stress described above, and these signs are compounded when the person becomes stressed out often.

Unless you are seriously ill or living in an unsustainable environment (plagued by famine, drought, war, pestilence, etc.), true life or death situations should be a rare occurrence in your life. In addition, most life or death situations are short-lived (temporary). Therefore, after the life or death situation has passed, you were either able to fight off the danger or to escape from the danger and are now safe, the PSNS is activated and brings the body back to its normal balance; the PSNS reverses the changes caused by the Stress Response.

However, many people have developed the bad habit of becoming stressed out regularly. Some people overreact to situations that are not life or death as if they are life or death on a daily basis, or even several times a day, or every week...too often. When a person becomes stressed out very often, the frequency of stressed out episodes do not allow enough time for the PSNS to bring the body back to balance. So one Stress Response runs into the next Stress Response, which runs into the next Stress Response, with no break in between for the PSNS to take over and allow the body, mind and emotions to calm down. Therefore, the Stress Response just keeps on working...and working. And while the Stress Response is of help to us in an true life or death crisis which may happen only once in a while, when there are no life or death situations, but yet the Stress Response is being triggered frequently, the negative effects of these false alarms can cause serious health problems, such as the ones described in the previous chapters[8].

You can see how health problems develop from ongoing activation of the Stress Response:

- The suppressed appetite can lead to poor nutrition, eating disorders and a weakened immune system.

- The diversion of blood from the stomach and intestines can lead to stomach and intestinal problems.

---

[8] There are more detrimental effects of the Stress Response on the physical body; we are only covering the main ones.

- Over secretion of acid by the stomach can lead to stomach (gastric) ulcers and chronic acid reflux.

- The elevated blood sugar (glucose) can lead to diabetes.

- The elevated blood pressure can lead to hypertension (high blood pressure)[6], which can lead to headaches, stroke, as well as kidney and heart disease; hypertension causes damage to blood vessels.

- The cholesterol that is released into the bloodstream can lead or contribute to high blood cholesterol over time.

- The effect of having the blood clot easily can lead to blood clot formation, which could cause a heart attack, stroke, or an embolism.

- Elevated levels of cortisol can lower immune function (suppress the immune system), which can predispose one to infections and has been associated with many conditions of ill health, including cancer.

- Adrenaline is that compound that the emergency doctor on TV shows always asks for when resuscitating a patient whose heart has stopped beating; it is also called epinephrine ("epi").

The doctor then injects the epinephrine into the patient's bloodstream or directly into the patient's heart, to cause the heart to start beating again; so, it's powerful stuff.

But what happens when this compound floods the body of person with a normal heartbeat, or even more serious, a person with heart disease or a stressed out person whose heartbeat is already racing from prior activation of the Stress Response?

It will cause the heart to beat faster (tachycardia), and it can also cause the heart to beat irregularly (an arrhythmia)[9/10] or the blood vessels of the heart to spasm, which can lead to a heart attack.

So, you can see the significant role that stress plays in both the very common and very serious conditions of ill health that plague our society, such as acid reflux, diabetes, high blood pressure, stroke, heart attacks[7], heart disease, etc.

It is important to realize and understand the relationship between stress and these conditions of ill health, because then it follows that therapies to heal these conditions should focus on not only taking medications to eliminate the symptoms of these conditions, but also on de-stressing.

---

[9] Vanoli E, Schwartz PJ. Sympathetic--parasympathetic interaction and sudden death. Basic Res Cardiol. 1990;85 Suppl 1:305-21. Review: **"...it has been shown that...sympathetic hyperactivity is arrhythmogenic..."**
[10] Schwartz PJ, La Rovere MT, Vanoli E. Autonomic nervous system and sudden cardiac death. Experimental basis and clinical observations for post-myocardial infarction risk stratification. Circulation. 1992 Jan;85(1 Suppl):I77-91. Review: **"sympathetic activation can trigger malignant arrhythmias, whereas vagal activity may exert a protective effect."**
(Note: "Sympathetic activation" refers to the SNS and "vagal activity" refers to the PSNS.)

Table 1: Summary of Effects of the Sympathetic Nervous System (Stress Response) and the Parasympathetic Nervous System (counters Stress Response):

Nervous System:	SNS	PSNS
Pulse/ Heart Rate	Increases	Decreases
Blood Pressure	Increases	Decreases
Sweating	Increases	Decreases
Eyes-Pupils	Dilates	Constricts
Eye lids	Open Widely	Relaxed & Droopy
Secretion of Digestive Juices	Decreases	Increases
Bowel Mobility	Decreases	Increases
Blood Glucose	Increases	Decreases
Lungs- air passages	Wide open	Constricted
Muscle tone	Increases	Decreases

Chapter 5: Understanding The Relationship Between Stress, High Blood Pressure, High Cholesterol, and other Common Illnesses

Stress versus Genetic Predisposition to Illness

Some people who are ill due to conditions caused by or associated with stress refuse to acknowledge that stress may be causing or exacerbating their symptoms or condition of ill health because medical research has found that some health conditions, such as heart disease, hypercholesterolemia (high cholesterol), and hypertension (high blood pressure), may have a genetic component. These persons believe that it is pointless to take measures to control their stress because the source of the illness is their genes. This type of reasoning also affects persons whose family members have a history of a certain disease. They feel that because everyone else in their family had a particular condition of ill health, it is inevitable that they too will get it...it's probably in their genes. Therefore, if they are going to get it, they are going to get it regardless of what they do...so why bother! But this is not true.

If you are genetically predisposed to a disease, you need to work harder to avoid getting it than someone who does not have a genetic predisposition.

Just because something is in your genes, and even if your parents or grandparents had it, does not mean you cannot do anything about it. Actually, it means the opposite. It means that because you are predisposed to that condition, you have to make sure you do everything reasonably possible to try to prevent getting that condition. For example, if it is in your genes to get fat, then you have to make sure you eat a healthy low fat diet and exercise. You cannot become fat if you do not take in calories in excess of what you are burning every day or if you burn off the excess calories by exercise.

As we saw in the previous chapter, many conditions of ill health have a direct association with the physiological effects that result from the activation of the Stress Response (e.g., adrenaline released into the blood during activation of the Stress Response can lead to a heart attack; increased stomach {gastric} acid production can lead to the development of acid reflux and stomach {gastric} ulcers, etc.). Also, recall the study discussed in the *Introduction* that showed a link between high increases in blood pressure due to the effects of stress in young adults and the likelihood of them developing hypertension (high blood pressure) when they reached middle age[8]. So if your family is genetically predisposed to heart disease, heart attacks, cancer, stroke, high blood pressure, high cholesterol, diabetes, eating disorders, etc., it becomes even more important for you to learn to de-stress and stop the Stress Response from being triggered falsely.

Stress, Cholesterol, Genetic Predisposition and Diet

High blood cholesterol is one of the conditions that has been linked to genetic predisposition. It is important to know that our bodies make cholesterol. Just as the Stress Response is beneficial in the right circumstances, the cholesterol that our bodies make under normal, healthy circumstances is beneficial for the physical body. It is needed for the normal functioning of the physical body, such as for the construction of our cells as well as other vital processes. But if the blood cholesterol level increases and remains high for a long period of time, it can damage the body, especially the heart and blood vessels.

Cholesterol is ONLY found in animals. It is NOT found in any plant or vegetable matter.

One point about cholesterol that many people do not know is that it is ONLY found in animals. It is NOT found in ANY plant or vegetable matter. Vegetarian diets that contain no animal products (non-dairy, no meat of any kind {including no fish and no seafood}, no eggs) have zero

('0') cholesterol and are specifically referred to as vegan diets.

Vegetarian-Vegan Foods: No ("0") Cholesterol

So, another source where people introduce cholesterol into their bodies is from eating animal products, such as meat, dairy products and eggs[11].

Animal Products Containing Cholesterol

In one medical study, participants who normally ate a vegetarian diet were fed meat for a period of four weeks to assess the effects of eating meat on raising the blood cholesterol level. After four weeks of eating a meat-inclusive diet, their cholesterol levels increased as much as 19% over the control levels (when they ate a vegetarian diet)[9]. Therefore, if one has a genetic predisposition for developing high cholesterol, has high blood cholesterol, or is stressed out (recall that activation of the Stress Response causes one's blood cholesterol to increase), it is common sense that one should stop putting more cholesterol into a highly susceptible or an already overloaded system. One

> In a medical study, vegetarians who were fed meat for four weeks had as much as a 19% increase in their blood cholesterol levels.

---

[11] About 15% comes from the diet, and 85% from what the body makes (Marieb, E., Essentials of Human Anatomy and Physiology, Benjamin/Cummings 2000)

If one has high cholesterol, it is common sense not to put more cholesterol into an already overloaded system.

Vegetarian diets have been scientifically shown to lower blood cholesterol levels.

Dr. Ornish scientifically showed that a vegetarian diet, de-stressing & exercise could reverse heart disease.

way to do this is to adopt a healthy balanced vegetarian diet (eating no meat, eggs or dairy products…i.e., a vegan diet). In addition, if one applies the tools of de-stressing, one would minimize or prevent the body from dumping cholesterol from its own storage reserves into the bloodstream in times of stress.

Many medical doctors and the pharmaceutical companies that make cholesterol lowering drugs emphasize that there are two sources of cholesterol that can contribute to high cholesterol, the cholesterol your own body makes and the cholesterol you eat. They use the argument that sometimes diet alone, even a low-fat diet, is not enough, so you must take drugs to lower your cholesterol, but at least on the commercials, they never mention that practicing de-stressing techniques and or eating a '0' cholesterol vegetarian diet could also lower your cholesterol. It has been medically-scientifically shown that a vegetarian diet can lower blood cholesterol[10]. Dr. Dean Ornish has scientifically shown that a low-fat vegetarian diet, stress management (de-stressing), and exercise can reverse heart disease, lower cholesterol and even lower blood pressure[11].

So, having a genetic predisposition for a specific condition of ill health only predisposes you to getting that condition, which means it makes it easier for you to get that condition as compared to someone else who does not have a genetic predisposition. However, it does not mean that you will get it or that you must get it. It also does not mean that if you do get that condition, you should give up on adopting healthy lifestyle modalities such as a low fat vegetarian diet, moderate exercise, de-stressing, etc., to minimize or relieve the symptoms, slow the course of the disease, and or heal oneself of the condition.

So, you have a great deal of influence over how a specific condition of ill health impacts you, in spite of having a genetic predisposition. You can be proactive and choose to make de-stressing a part of your life before the effects of stress trigger or worsen an illness, which may take some time to reverse and heal, or not be able to be healed at all. As the saying goes, an ounce of prevention is worth a pound of cure.

The Cycle of Stress and Illness

Another connection between stress and ill health is that not only can stress cause or be associated with conditions of ill health, but also, when one has an illness, one's capacity to handle situations that one finds difficult or challenging is generally reduced. Thus, one becomes more susceptible to overreacting emotionally and falsely triggering the Stress Response, i.e., getting stressed out. This further compounds the negative effects of stress on the illness. Therefore, illness can be caused by or associated with stress, and also can be a trigger for more stress, and that stress can further worsen the illness.

Stress   Illness

So, even though you may find it very challenging or difficult to muster the effort to practice de-stressing techniques when you are ill, it is important to do so. De-stressing tools have been medically-scientifically shown to be beneficial in several conditions of ill health, including headaches, back pain, stroke, heart disease, etc.[12] Consult with a de-stressing expert and choose whichever technique(s) you are able to practice comfortably in your condition of ill health (with the approval of your physician), and practice consistently.

> De-stressing tools have been scientific-ally shown to be of benefit in certain condi-tions of ill health.

Chapter 6: Vegetarian Diet and Stress

Many scientific researches in the medical community document numerous health benefits of vegetarian diets[13]. Both the United States and Canadian dietitian associations are in agreement that vegetarian diets can be beneficial in the prevention and treatment of some diseases:

> *"It is the position of the American Dietetic Association and Dietitians of Canada that appropriately planned vegetarian diets are healthful, nutritionally adequate, and provide health benefits in the prevention and treatment of certain diseases."*[14]

In addition, the American Dietetic Association states the following about vegetarian-vegan (containing no animal products) diets:

> *"Well-planned vegan and other types of vegetarian diets are appropriate for all stages of the life cycle, including during pregnancy, lactation, infancy, childhood, and adolescence."*[15]

Documented health benefits of vegetarian diets include: reversal of heart disease[16], decreased blood pressure in hypertensive patients[17], reduced heart disease[18], reduced cancer risk[19], improved glycemic (glucose, blood sugar) control and improved cardiovascular risk factors for people with type 2 diabetes[20], slower progression of prostate cancer[21], etc.

There are many documented health benefits of a vegetarian diet in the medical literature.

Considering the cycle of stress and illness just described in the previous chapter, the health promoting aspects of a vegetarian diet certainly make it an effective tool in relieving and preventing stress. Some conditions of ill health associated with stress may be prevented, minimized, or possibly even healed by following a healthy low-fat vegetarian diet.

Vegetarian diets[12] have been incorporated into medical research lifestyle programs for managing heart disease[22]. These lifestyle programs incorporate different modalities that promote physical and mental health, such as a low-fat vegetarian diet, moderate exercise, stress-management training, group support, and stopping smoking. Results of these studies have documented both physical and mental (better coping, less stress) benefits in participants. Because these studies apply different approaches to health at the same time, it is difficult to say which modality caused a particular benefit, but there is a bigger point here. While these studies do not conclusively state that a low-fat vegetarian diet alone decreases stress or reverses heart disease, etc., what they do say is that one can derive substantial physical and mental health benefits from a lifestyle that incorporates eating a low-fat vegetarian diet, moderate exercise, stress-management training, group support, and smoking cessation. Because all of these lifestyle modalities are individually advocated by health experts for a healthy life, does it really matter which one causes what? Why not just practice all of them and enjoy a healthier and more stress free life?

Vegetarian diets have physical health benefits, but they may also have "peace" benefits. In the medical study discussed in the previous chapter where participants who normally ate a vegetarian diet were fed meat for a period of four weeks to assess the effects of eating meat on raising the blood cholesterol level, the participants were also evaluated for changes in mood. Not only did four weeks of eating a meat-inclusive diet increase their cholesterol levels as much as 19% over the control levels (when they ate a

---

[12] Some of these studies allowed egg whites and non-fat yogurt as part of the diet.

vegetarian diet), but the participants also exhibited "significantly higher" scores on the evaluation of five adverse mood factors: anxiety, depression, anger, fatigue and confusion, and a lower score for the positive factor, vigor, during this period[23]. In other words, they experienced more anxiety, depression, anger, fatigue, confusion and physical tiredness (reduced vigor). Note that these five adverse mood factors that were significantly higher in this study, as well as the reduced vigor that was noted, are on the list of signs of stress in Chapter 8, #1 *Recognize Signs Of A Stress Attack*. So, the participants experienced more stress when they were unknowingly fed a meat inclusive diet as compared to when they were unknowingly fed a vegetarian diet.

Medical study finds link between some signs of stress and eating meat.

Some human medical doctors, nutritionists, naturopathic physicians, as well as de-stressing (stress management) therapists, experts and teachers, including myself, are not surprised by the above findings showing a link between eating meat and signs of stress. One reason is based on the comparative anatomy, physiology and biochemistry of herbivores (animals that eat only plants), carnivores (animals that primarily eat meat), and omnivores (animals that eat both meat and plants) that clearly shows that humans are more herbivores than anything else. Dr Milton Mills, M.D., compared 19 different features (both anatomical and physiological – i.e., teeth structure, jaw movement, length of intestines, pH of stomach, digestive enzymes, etc.) of carnivores, omnivores and herbivores, and humans fell into the herbivorous category for each parameter[24]. Therefore, just as if you were to put the wrong fuel into your car, it would stress the system (mess things up), if not right away, after a while, putting the wrong fuel into the human mind-body system will also stress this system (mess things up), and result in conditions of ill-health, including stress.

Compara-tive studies by Dr Mills, M.D. shows that humans are vegetar-ians.

There is yet a more subtle consideration with regard to the above study that linked eating a meat-inclusive diet to stress (i.e., anxiety, anger, depression, confusion, fatigue and lack of vigor). On a philosophical level, de-stressing can be defined as finding peace, and eating a plant-based diet is more in line with peace than eating the meat of slaughtered animals. When animals are slaughtered for meat, the procedure is not gentle. The animals end up being in a life or death struggle. I experienced this first hand, because in addition to being a pastoral counselor and a de-stressing and Yoga instructor, I am also a veterinarian. As part of my pre-veterinary curriculum, I took some animal science courses where I spent time in slaughterhouses observing the process by which animals are slaughtered for human food.

The Stress Response is not unique to human beings. Other animals also experience it, perhaps even more intensely than humans, because due to their environment, they are always at risk of facing a natural predator. So, the Stress Response of the animals that are being slaughtered is activated...after all, they are in a real life or death struggle[25]. Thus, their tissues are under the effects of the stress hormones at the time of their death.

Some human medical doctors, nutritionists, naturopathic physicians, as well as de-stressing (stress management) therapists, experts and teachers, including myself, also feel that consuming the meat of animals that are slaughtered is unhealthy because their bodies are under the effects of the Stress Response...and this may somehow activate or perpetuate a false alarm triggering of the Stress Response in the person eating the meat. Recall the medical study above where the participants experienced increased signs of stress (anxiety, depression, anger, fatigue, confusion, and reduced vigor) when they ate meat as compared to when they ate a vegetarian diet.

Furthermore, many of the animals that are raised for human food live in conditions that are very unnatural and sometimes unsanitary, overcrowded and inhumane...so their Stress Responses are chronically activated, over a long period of time, well before they are slaughtered. Considering the adverse effects of ongoing activation of the Stress Response in people, it certainly does not seem that the meat and other food products from these animals can be completely healthy. Some health food stores sell meat and other food products from animals that are raised in settings that are more natural and on more natural (grass) diets, however, there is still the issue of the activation of the Stress Response associated with the slaughtering of the animals.

A study[26] of mice that were placed in an environment with various olfactory (related to smell) stimuli showed that they displayed greater anxiety when they encountered fecal matter from cats fed a carnivorous diet than cats fed a vegetarian diet. So, there may be even subtler effects of human beings eating a meat inclusive diet that are yet to be explored by behavioral and medical science. However, there is already enough medically sound scientific data to support the health benefits of a vegetarian diet.

Regardless of if you change to a vegetarian diet or not, you will derive benefits from the other de-stressing tools presented in this book. So, do not be put off by this discussion of vegetarianism. It is being presented as one more de-stressing tool option.

Transitioning to a vegetarian diet also is a process that can take time, depending on the individual. It may even begin with resistance to the idea. So, if this is not something you feel you are ready for, just leave it alone for now...it may be something you come back to. It is certainly something I would recommend you try if you are stressed out.

Whenever anyone says that there is no way they can become a vegetarian, I tell them if I can do it, they can too, because I had the worst reputation in my family for eating just about any type of meat product...even the very unusual ones. And for me, what triggered the change initially was a health issue.

My own research led me to conclude that a vegetarian-vegan diet is the diet that is most suited to the human anatomy and physiology, especially that I had studied the anatomy and physiology of both herbivores (cows, etc.) and carnivores (dogs, cats, etc.) as a veterinary student.

In addition to my recommendation and the researches and references I have provided in this book, you may wish to do your own experiment and implement a vegetarian-vegan diet for a certain period of time (e.g., three months) and notice how you feel.

Of course, you should consult your health care practitioner and seek counseling from a knowledgeable dietitian or nutritionist before making changes to your diet, especially if you have medical conditions of ill health, such as diabetes. You also need to learn about eating a healthy well-balanced low-fat vegetarian diet, because it is also possible to eat a highly processed junk-food or high-fat vegetarian diet.

I also recommend you read books and do your own research on vegetarian-vegan diets and on making the transition to a vegetarian-vegan diet in a healthy and safe manner. Some vegetarian resources are provided at the end of this book.

Part 3: Understanding De-stressing

Chapter 7: How De-stressing Works

Breaking the Stress Habit

De-stressing has three main parts. One part is learning how not to trigger the Stress Response in situations that are not a matter of life or death. Another part is learning how to stop the Stress Response once it has been falsely triggered. The third part is how to recover from or minimize the effects of the Stress Response if you were not able to prevent it or stop it. There is some overlap in the de-stressing tools presented in these three parts.

This section of the book, *Part 3, Basic Tools for De-stressing*, will first cover tools to stop the Stress Response once it has been falsely triggered, followed by techniques that will enable you to recover from or minimize the effects of the Stress Response if you were not able to prevent it or stop it. It will then address how to not trigger the Stress Response in situations that are not a matter of life or death.

The discussion on how to stop the Stress Response once it has been falsely triggered is presented first because as you have been practicing being stressed out for some time, your mind is well trained in this pattern of reacting to life. Therefore, as discussed above, that behavior pattern will still continue, though to a lesser degree and or with less intensity, for some time.

In other words, it has become a bad habit, and because it takes time to break a bad habit and retrain the thought and feeling processes to develop a new and good habit, you will continue to experience some amount of stress, because you will continue to react to situations that are not life or death as if they are…for a while still. Therefore, you need to be very patient with yourself and with the process of

Be patient. Realize that it is going to take some time to break the old (bad) habit of becoming stressed out.

becoming proficient at de-stressing, and not give up on it before it has had time to become established as a habit.

Be patient; do not give up before de-stressing becomes a (good) habit.

The more you use these tools of de-stressing and apply them in situations when you feel stress coming on, the more proficient you will become in de-stressing. You will eventually get to the point that de-stressing happens just as automatically as getting stressed out now happens. Just think about when you were a child and you were learning to ride a bike, how it seemed to be such a challenge in the beginning. You may have even fallen down a few times and bruised yourself. But once you "got it" and kept on practicing, you became better and better, until one day you were able to get on the bike and not think twice about all the different little points of learning to ride…it came to you automatically. This is true for learning any skill. In the beginning, the pace is slow, the intensity you need to apply is great, and it is fraught with errors and challenges. However, if you continue to apply yourself and make it through this phase, then the rewards are forthcoming…you become proficient at the skill, so much so that you can perform it naturally. Similarly, de-stressing can be thought of as acquiring a skill.

There is such an emphasis in Western culture on "life" (work, family, relationships) being stressful, that it may be difficult for you to see how your thoughts have anything to do with your feeling stressed out. But as we discussed above, they have everything to do with feeling stressed out. The reason you may not recognize it is because you have been overreacting to situations for so long, that it has become a bad habit, and happens automatically now.

A habit is when we have done the behavior repeatedly for so long that it goes into the unconscious mind and the unconscious mind takes over. Most people do not have easy access to their unconscious mind, so it just seems like the behavior is happening on its own and you have no control over it. The way the unconscious mind takes over when we have learned something to the point that it becomes a habit can be a good thing when the habits are good habits that benefit us, like learning to play the piano, eating healthily, exercising, etc. Imagine if every time pianists played the piano, they had to think about every musical note consciously. They would not be able to play very fast, or very well.

So, the key is to develop good habits, which then become a positive foundation of good thoughts in the unconscious mind that can help us automatically, without having to think about them consciously all the time and put forth conscious effort to put them into action.

When we have already developed bad habits, one may think that the key is to break the bad habit. While working on breaking the bad habit is part of the process, the key to succeeding is really to develop a good habit to replace the bad habit, so that there is no need for the bad habit anymore. The mind tries to find situations of comfort and happiness. If it has a new better habit that will make it feel happier to use in place of an old bad habit, it will use the new better habit, and the old bad habit will fade away from disuse. Therefore, your greatest emphasis should be on practicing these new techniques, rather than being disturbed by the old habits continuing to come out. At some point your practice of the de-stressing techniques will overtake the expression of the bad stress habit, and you will have conscious control over if you become stressed out or not. Then with more practice of the techniques, de-stressing will become an unconscious process, a habit, and happen automatically, and replace the bad stress habit.

> The key to breaking a bad habit is to develop a good habit to replace it.

You have the potential to be totally stress-free.

So, although you may not think that you think yourself into stress, you do! You must accept this, because this is the key to changing. You can change the way you think. You can change the way you think consciously, and also the consolidated thoughts that have become habits in the unconscious mind. This means you have the potential to be totally stress-free.

The Mind-Body Connection

An important de-stressing tool is to become aware that you are NOT in a life or death situation.

An important tool for minimizing or eliminating inappropriate stress (false alarm activation of the Stress Response) is to develop awareness that the situation you are dealing with IS NOT a life or death situation. This is the basis for de-stressing, because if you don't differentiate between a false alarm and a real life or death situation, then you won't be able to prevent yourself from overreacting or gain control over your intense emotions in a difficult but non-life-threatening situation.

The mind (thoughts) and physical body communicate so closely with each other that they can be regarded as one unit; this is why I am referring to them as the body-mind complex.

Let's demonstrate this close relationship between the physical body and mind (thoughts). Think about a lime.

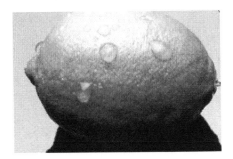

Now, visualize the following: *Smell the lime. Cut the lime in half. Now bite into the lime and taste the limejuice.*

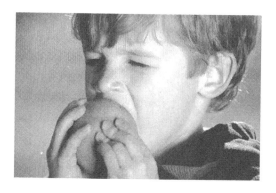

Although all of this imagination was only in the form of thoughts, i.e., you did not actually taste an actual lime, you probably found yourself puckering your lips and even salivating a bit.

That illustrates the power the mind can have on the body and the very quick and precise intercommunications that take place between the body and mind. These communications between the mind and physical body work both ways, from the mind to the body and also from the body to the mind. The tools of de-stressing take advantage of this fact of the two-way communications between the body and mind.

Therefore, if you can get your body to calm down (e.g., by breathing deeply or applying the other de-stressing tools below, etc.), the mind will follow. Alternatively, if you can get your mind to calm down (e.g., by becoming aware that you are not thinking correctly about the situation, that it is not a life or death situation), then the body will also relax.

The intercommunications and interactions that occur between the mind and body form the basis of another key to de-stressing, because at times you may find it easier to

> De-stressing tools make use of the bi-directional communica-tion between the body and mind.

work with the mind, and at other times you may find it easier to work with the physical body, but either way you can "relax" and know you are de-stressing both your physical body and mind.

> Due to the mind-body connection, relaxing the mind will relax the body, and vice versa.

It is generally easier to work with de-stressing tools that focus on the physical body when one is stressed, especially in the beginning, because if one could handle one's mental-emotional overreaction, one would do that automatically and not even get upset in the first place.

So, this is why a lot of de-stressing tools focus on de-stressing from the level of the physical body, allowing the mind to follow. In this book, I also focus on de-stressing from the mental level as well, by recognizing your overreaction and changing your thoughts, so that you can work on de-stressing from both the physical and mental levels.

Eventually, as you become more sensitive to your thoughts and recognize how they promote stress and how they can minimize or eliminate stress, and as you learn how to think correctly about your circumstances as well as work to eliminate the seeds of stress in your unconscious mind, you will be able to just change your thoughts to de-stress.

> You must know it is possible to be stress-free.

When your mind becomes established in the "new" de-stressed thought process, then stress won't even be an issue any more...you can be stress-free. You must know this is possible; it will be discussed in Chapter 10.

Chapter 8: Tools of De-stressing Part One - Stopping a False Activation of the Stress Response

Summary Of Tools To Stop The Stress Response Once It Has Been Falsely Activated:

1) Recognize the signs of a stress attack.
2) Think correctly – Realize it's not a matter of life or death.
3) Practice the Deep Breathing technique.
4) Eat healthy meals...do not skip meals; vegetarian-vegan diet.
5) Change your environment.
6) Exercise.
7) Change your conscious thought process.
8) Any combination of #1-7.

1) Recognize Signs Of A Stress Attack:

Recall some of the early warning signs of stress[27]:

- *Anger*
- *Irritability*
- *Inability to control violent impulses*
- *Defensive*
- *Arrogant*
- *Argumentative*
- *Rebellious*
- *Insecurity*
- *Sadness*
- *Feeling suspicious*
- *Preoccupied*
- *the "Blahs" - apathy*

- *Grandiosity (exaggerating the importance of your activities to yourself and others)*
- *Anxiety*
- *Mental fatigue*
- *Overcompensation or Denial*
- *Restlessness*
- *Agitated*
- *Avoiding things*
- *Doing things to extremes (alcoholism, etc.)*
- *Not handling one's finances well*
- *Frequent illness*
- *Physical exhaustion*

Physical signs of stress that occur almost immediately after a false activation of the Stress Response (SNS), and which you should be alert to observe yourself for, include:

- Pounding Heart...your heart pounding (beating hard) in your chest
- Racing Heart...your heart is beating very fast
- Feeling pressure in your head or chest
- Rapid and shallow breathing
- Breaking out in a sweat, sweaty palms
- Cold hands
- Feeling weak and shaky in the legs
- Tightening or tensing of your muscles

Other signs of stress you may experience include:

- Getting stomach cramps (butterflies, feeling nauseous)
- Intestinal cramping, urge to have a bowel movement
- Not feeling like eating (suppressed appetite), overeating
- Urge to urinate

- Not able to sleep very well (if your mind-body complex thinks there is danger lurking nearby, the Stress Response will keep you awake to watch out for this danger, so insomnia is another effect of the Stress Response)

Therefore, if you find yourself experiencing any of these signs, you may be experiencing stress. The earlier you can become aware of the onset of these signs, the sooner you can begin to apply the tools of de-stressing to interrupt and stop the Stress Response, and the less stressed out you will become. However, these signs may also be associated with other conditions of ill health, so it is best to consult with your health care practitioner before attributing these signs only to stress.

By learning to recognize the signs of stress, you can stop a false activation of the SR.

I would like you to take a few moments to place a check mark by or write in a notepad or journal each of the above signs of stress that you have experienced. You can also include other signs you have experienced that may not be listed above.

Now, consider if you have a typical pattern that your body follows in responding to stress, and make an asterisk mark by or write down the signs you most commonly experience whenever you have a stress attack.

For example, do you become irritated and lash out or become quiet and preoccupied and get the "blahs"? Do you get stomach cramps, become sad, not feel like eating and have difficulty sleeping? You may have experienced all the different signs of stress listed above at different times, and you may find that your body-mind complex reacts in a certain way or pattern a lot of the times, which includes only a few of the above signs.

Also, consider if you have a pattern of escalation. What I mean by this is, as you continue to get worked up about a situation, reacting to a non-life-threatening situation as if it were one, is there a pattern to the signs you experience as your upset and fearful response escalates? Maybe you become irritated or angry first, then you experience a tightening of the muscles in your chest, then you feel a tightening in your stomach, then stomach cramps, then the "blahs," then sadness, etc.

> Observe yourself and try to recognize the onset of the signs of stress.

Start to observe how your mind-body complex reacts when you feel stressed and notice which signs of stress predominate. When you know the signs of stress and can recognize your most common pattern of reacting to stress, then you can consciously start to become aware of and identify when you are becoming stressed out, and apply your de-stressing tools right then and there.

If you cannot figure out your usual pattern, ask your family or close friends. They have most likely observed how you react when you are stressed out, and can share this information with you, especially if they have ever made statements like the following to you about your behavior in a certain situation: *"So what's new...you always act like that."* or *"Well, that's typical!"*

> Learning and recognizing the signs of stress in yourself are important de-stressing tools.

So, learning the mental-emotional and physiological (bodily) signs of stress, and then recognizing the signs of stress in yourself, are important in the process of de-stressing, because then you have the opportunity to recognize the onset of a stress attack, a false alarm activation of the Stress Response, and stop it.

2) Think Correctly – Realize It's Not A Matter of Life or Death:

This is an expansion of #1 above. Use this tool anytime you recognize that a false alarm of the Stress Response is underway. Because it is your wrong thinking about the situation that is triggering the Stress Response, you can become so sensitive in observing yourself for signs of stress that you can even recognize the emerging stress-thought process and change that, before the Stress Response has a chance to be activated, thus preventing the stress from occurring. Even if you have not yet been able to change the unconscious thoughts that produced the habit of responding to non-life-threatening situations as if they are, you can use the following technique of substitution to disable the emerging stress-thought process. Applying this technique of thinking correctly about the situation at hand will chip away at the old habit of wrong thinking and eventually replace it.

> To change an unwanted thought, substitute an opposite thought.

Technique for changing a wrong thought process:

Substitute the opposite thought process.

So, if you recognize that your thoughts or emerging thoughts are or will be leading you in the direction of a stress attack, that is, reacting to a non-life or death situation in an emotionally upset and fearful manner, or if the Stress Response is already activated, substitute the opposite thought process; remind yourself of the truth of your circumstances, that it is not a life or death situation. You can say something to yourself like:

While I find this situation difficult to handle at the moment, it is NOT a life or death situation. I am safe. So, relax. Breathe deeply. Calm down. Calm down and then approach the situation again from this calmer perspective....this situation is difficult, but it is not a matter of life or death! I have worked through difficulties before and will work through this one. So, I don't need to be stressed out over it.

You may have to repeat such affirmations or statements to yourself, repeatedly, for a long time, to counteract the incorrect but habitual thoughts that keep trying to surface about the situation being some sort of life-threatening crisis when it is not.

3) Deep Breathing Technique:

The Deep Breathing technique, also called the *Three-Part Breath*, or the *Deep Yogic Breath*, is especially good, because you can practice it and no one but you will know that you are de-stressing. You can practice it in situations where you do not want to disrupt the unfolding events, such as if you on your way to a job interview, giving a lecture or presentation, or if someone like your boss or teacher is yelling at you and you do not want to leave the room. This is a very effective and quiet de-stressing tool to stop the Stress Response[13]. Dr Sandra McLanahan, M.D.[28], a medical doctor who studies the Stress Response and teaches de-stressing techniques says that it is physiologically impossible for a person to breathe deeply and remain stressed out. This is because there is a link between the Respiratory (breathing) System and the Nervous System called the Hering-Breuer reflex. When you breathe deeply, the SNS-Stress Response is disrupted and

> The Deep Breathing Technique allows you to de-stress in situations where you need to be discreet.

---

[13]Brown RP, Gerbarg PL. Sudarshan Kriya Yogic breathing in the treatment of stress, anxiety, and depression. Part II--clinical applications and guidelines. J Altern Complement Med. 2005 Aug;11(4):711-7. Review: **"Yogic breathing is a unique method for balancing the autonomic nervous system and influencing psychological and stress-related disorders."**

the PSNS is activated to cause your mind-body complex to automatically go into a relaxed state.

This makes common sense. If shallow and rapid breathing is associated with the Stress Response, with a life or death situation, then the opposite, slow and deep breathing, should send a signal to the Nervous System that you are not in a life or death situation, and the body-mind complex should calm down. This is exactly what breathing slowly and deeply does; it calms down the body-mind complex. The internal conversation within the Nervous System probably goes something like this:

> Deep Breathing short-circuits the falsely activated SR.

Hmm! I don't feel that shallow and rapid breathing anymore. Am I no longer in danger? I must be no longer in danger, because that deep and slow breathing is continuing. If I am out of danger, I can relax. Ok, time to turn off the Stress Response-SNS and to gear up the PSNS to relax, as I am no longer in danger.

So, the Deep Breathing technique short circuits the falsely activated Stress Response and stops its effects. You will feel calm, relaxed and peaceful soon after you begin to practice it.

Before practicing the Deep Breathing technique, it is important that you are breathing properly to begin with, as the Deep Breathing technique is a variation of Proper Breathing. Most people in the modern world do not know how to breathe properly. Most people (especially males) have learned to breathe by pushing out the chest (see Fig. A below) in a "manly" or "macho" fashion.

> Most people do not know how to breathe correctly.

This way of breathing decreases the amount of air and oxygen taken into the body. This can impact one's health, because if one is not taking enough oxygen into the body to support its needs, then the tissues and the organs will not be

Incorrect breathing can deprive the body of oxygen.

able to function properly, causing or perpetuating conditions of ill health. Thus, due to improper breathing, one may be depriving the body of one of its basic needs, i.e., air (oxygen), as discussed above in Chapter 3.

Proper Breathing, also called "Belly Breathing" or "Abdominal Breathing" is the proper way to breathe. It is how we are supposed to breathe; it's our natural breath…just observe a sleeping baby. Although it is called Belly Breathing, we do not have lungs in our belly. Our lungs are in our chest. But this technique works with the diaphragm, a horizontal muscle that separates our chest (lungs and heart, etc.) up above, from our abdomen or belly (stomach, liver, intestines, etc.) below. It is our main breathing muscle. Proper or Belly Breathing allows this muscle to work effectively and efficiently to provide oxygen to the body and get rid of waste products.

Belly breathing is our natural breath.

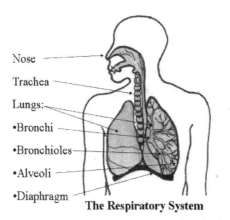

Nose
Trachea
Lungs:
•Bronchi
•Bronchioles
•Alveoli
•Diaphragm

The Respiratory System

Drawing by Oronde Reid

Proper breathing occurs naturally when we lay on our back.

When we lie down, we tend to breathe deeper and slower, and especially if we lie on our back, proper breathing comes to us naturally. This is another reason why lying down generally makes us feel relaxed. But because we train ourselves from a very young age, mostly unconsciously, to be stressed out, our breathing becomes more shallow and rapid as we grow older and become more and more stressed out, sometimes to the point that the breathing muscles weaken from disuse. So, when you begin to practice any breathing technique, initially practice only for a short time, and gradually build up, so you won't strain the breathing muscles that have not been used much recently.

Your posture also affects your breathing. During the course of your day, try to keep your back straight and not slouch forward as much as possible, because slouching forward decreases your capacity to breathe properly. Also, many people wear tight fitting clothes that restrict the free movement of the belly area, and Proper Breathing; instead, wear clothing that is loose in the belly area, so you can breathe properly throughout the day. Due to the movement of the belly (abdomen) with each breath, Proper or Belly Breathing also massages the internal organs in the abdomen (stomach, intestines, liver, etc.) and therefore promotes good circulation to those organs.

> Your posture affects your breathing. Avoid slouching forward to promote proper breathing

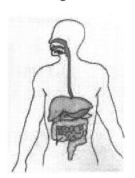

Organs of the Abdomen

Thus, Belly Breathing, in and of itself, will go a long way towards promoting health, releasing stress, and keeping you from becoming stressed out. But, if it is not enough to keep you de-stressed, and you recognize the signs of stress building up and know that you are becoming stressed out, then shift to the Deep Breathing Technique described below.

Instruction for Proper Breathing (Belly or Abdominal Breathing):

This form of breathing is to be practiced at all times. This should be your natural breath.

Evaluate how you breathe: To evaluate how you breathe, sit back in a straight back chair with your feet flat on the floor. Place the palm of one hand on your chest, and the palm of the other hand on your belly, and breathe for a few moments. Where do you feel most of the movement occurring...in your chest or in your belly? Next, evaluate when you breathe in, how does the belly move with the in breath (inhalation). Does it move in or out with each inhalation?

If most of the movement is occurring in your chest, you are breathing incorrectly, as in Fig. A, below. Also, if your belly is moving **in** with the **in breath**, you are breathing incorrectly. See Figs. B and C for how to breathe properly.

> If your belly moves in when you inhale, you are breathing incorrectly.

Proper Breathing Step 1: Breathe in through your nostrils and push the belly out...swelling it out like a balloon. (see Fig. B below).

Proper Breathing Step 2: Breathe out through your nostrils and pull the belly in. (see Fig. C below).

Continue to breathe in and out as described in Steps 1 and 2.

Fig. A: Incorrect "Chest" Breathing

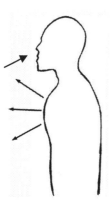

Figs. B & C: Correct: Proper "Belly" Breathing Technique

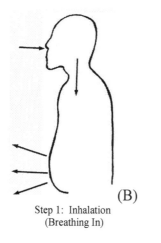

(B)

Step 1: Inhalation
(Breathing In)

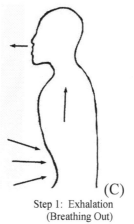

(C)

Step 1: Exhalation
(Breathing Out)

Deep Breathing Technique (The Three-Part or Yogic Breath):

Five important points:

1) Wear loose fitting clothing so that you can freely move the belly (abdomen) in and out.

2) Do not hold the breath.

3) Do not strain or force the breath on either the inhalation or exhalation. Inhale and exhale only to your capacity, and allow your capacity to slowly build up with increasing practice.

4) When practicing seated, be sure that your back is straight, and that you are sitting back enough so as not to put pressure on your belly.

5) Except as noted, you will be breathing through the nostrils. The nostrils filter the air we breathe as well as humidify and warm the air. When we breathe through the mouth, these benefits are by-passed.

Let's begin:

Deep Breathing Inhalation:

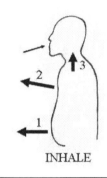

INHALE

Step 1: Breathe in (inhale) gently, steadily and slowly while pushing the belly out as described in the Proper Breathing technique above.

Step 2: Continue to inhale a little deeper filling the lungs in the chest area as you expand the chest outwards a bit.

Step 3: Continue to inhale a bit deeper still, allowing the shoulders to rise up a little, naturally, without strain, filling the area of the lungs under the shoulders.

Deep Breathing Exhalation (a reversal of the Inhalation):

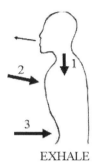

EXHALE

Step 1: Breathe out (exhale) gently, steadily and slowly, first letting the air out from the top of the lungs, releasing the shoulders as you do so (allow the shoulders to drop down a little, in a natural way, as you begin to exhale).

Step 2: Next, continue to exhale gently, steadily and slowly as you let the air out from the middle lung area, allowing the chest to deflate.

Step 3: Then exhale further by pulling the belly in, expelling all remaining air from the lungs, as described above in the Proper Breathing exercise.

This is one round of Deep Breathing. Proceed to Step 1 of Inhalation to continue practicing the technique.

Note On The Exhalation: In the beginning of your practice, it is all right if the exhalation is the same length as the inhalation or even shorter. Be sure to control your exhalation so that it is soft and smooth. As you progress in this practice, try to slow down the exhalation until it is twice as long as the time it took for the inhalation. It is best to allow your capacity to gradually build up. It is more important for you to keep the breath even and smooth, and not hold the breath or strain yourself as you exhale, than to force the exhalation to be twice as long as the inhalation.

Practicing The Deep Breathing Technique:

Although the Deep Breathing technique is given in a series of three steps each for the inhalation and exhalation, work to merge the three steps and make the Deep Three-Part Breath one smooth inhalation followed by one smooth exhalation, in an alternating pattern. This becomes easier with practice.

Start by practicing the Deep Breathing technique 5 minutes two or three times a day, and building up to about 10-20 minutes twice a day, and of course, whenever you recognize the onset of the signs of stress or are feeling stressed out.

Practice in a comfortable seated position, with your back straight. If you are sitting in a chair, place your feet flat on the floor, and allow your palms to rest gently on your lap.

Whenever you just want to relax and are in a place where you can lie down, you can just lie on your back, keeping your spine straight, supporting the little curve under your neck with a towel or small cloth, and breathe deeply, using the Deep Breathing technique to promote relaxation within your body and mind.

In the beginning, you will find it easier to practice the Deep Breathing technique lying down on your back.

You will note it is easier to practice the Deep Breathing technique lying down on your back, as it is merely building on Proper Breathing, which occurs naturally in this position. The only consideration is that you may become so relaxed you may drift into sleep. So, this is a great technique to practice at night when you want to go to sleep and to promote a peaceful night's sleep.

Additional Tips for Practicing Deep Breathing When You are Stressed Out:

When you are not in a formal setting, you can start this practice by exhaling completely through your open mouth as though you are letting out a big sigh, while pulling your belly in towards the spine.

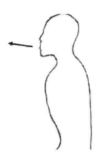

This will empty the lungs more effectively than just exhaling through your nose, removing stale air from the smaller air passages. After exhaling through your open mouth, proceed to Step 1 of the Deep Breathing Inhalation, and continue with your mouth closed, breathing only through your nostrils for the rest of the practice.

Also, when you feel stressed out, if you are able to find a place to be alone and quiet, you can practice this breathing technique with your eyes closed. Closing the eyes is another way to assure the SNS that you are not in danger, because if you were in danger, you certainly would not have your eyes closed. You would have them wide open to evaluate how to handle the danger.

Moreover, if you are somewhere you can lie down flat on your back to practice the Deep Breathing technique, this will further assure the SNS that you really are not in a life or death situation, because if danger were lurking about, you would not lie down on your back; you would sit up or stand up and be vigilant. So laying down further signals the Nervous System that you are in a safe environment, and therefore it can shut off the Stress Response and activate the PSNS.

4) Eat Healthy Meals:

When you are in a state of stress, generally your appetite will be poor, and therefore you will find it easier to skip meals. You may also experience abdominal cramps because of the stress. Yet, you should not skip meals. Try to eat something healthy at each meal, even if you can't get yourself to eat a full meal. Try some oatmeal for breakfast, or an apple. Oatmeal is very good for the Nervous System and very grounding.

If you deprive yourself of food, you will be reinforcing the Stress Response, because to the SNS, your not eating is consistent with your being in a dangerous situation, a life or death situation. In other words, by not eating, you are telling your SNS that you are in a dangerous life or death situation and are not in a position to safely eat. As a result, the SNS will keep activating the Stress Response. On the other hand, if you eat, you will be telling the Nervous System that you are not in a dangerous life or death situation, and therefore signaling it to stop the Stress Response and activate the PSNS, which will allow you to release stress.

Eating healthy meals will stop false activation of the SR and release stress.

But overeating can also occur as a reaction to feeling stressed out, due to the need to feel nurtured; this is discussed below in Chapter 9, #2. If you feel the urge to munch between meals, choose healthy snacks that will also limit your caloric intake, such as carrot or celery sticks, while implementing your de-stressing program.

5) Change Your Environment:

You can change your environment if you are in a position to do so and if you are too upset to practice the Deep Breathing technique. Recall that it is easier in the beginning to use de-stressing tools that are more physical, rather than the more subtle ones such as breathing or changing one's thoughts. So, go for a walk if you can. Go somewhere that you will be safe and can be by yourself. If you are at work, just walking outside of the building to take a few deep breaths of fresh air may be enough to stop the Stress Response.

In the beginning, you will find it easier to practice de-stressing tools that are more physical in nature.

A natural setting can help you calm down and de-stress.

For some people, going out to a natural setting such as to a park, a lake, or the beach helps them to feel safe and calm and will stop the Stress Response. If you are at home, you can try going to a different room than the person you are reacting to in a stressful manner, until you calm down.

6) Exercise:

Exercise can also be used to assist with de-stressing. But it should be light to moderate, should promote deep breathing, should not cause excessive panting or hyperventilating, and should not expose the physical body to extreme changes in temperature or extreme pain or injury[29]. In addition to the distraction it provides, exercise allows the nervous "stress–energy" to be dissipated. Walking for about 20-30 minutes is a good form of exercise that meets the above criteria, and would also provide a change of environment discussed in #5 above.

> To promote de-stressing, exercise should be light to moderate in intensity.

7) Change Your Conscious Thoughts:

You can change the thoughts in your conscious mind. You can turn your mind to positive or happy thoughts, which will then send messages to the Nervous System that you are not in a life or death situation, and stop the Stress Response. Positive or happy thoughts can include prayer or repeating a mantra/hekau.[14] You can recite positive affirmations. You can also visualize a happy occasion.

> Thinking positive thoughts or visualizing a happy occasion can stop the false activation of the SR and allow you to de-stress.

There is a saying about how situations generally work themselves out that goes: *things are generally never as good as you hoped, or as bad as you feared.* So, most situations usually resolve themselves in some acceptable way and therefore, you don't need to approach a non-life or death situation you find difficult or challenging as a life or death issue. You don't need to anticipate or fear the worse. Just think of how many challenging or difficult situations you have already faced, and how they have all worked themselves out in some way, usually the best way possible

---

[14] Hekau is an Ancient African word for mantra.

when you take into account all the different parameters of the circumstances. So, have a positive outlook.

Even life or death situations can be handled more effectively with a calm mind and positive attitude. Because of the mind-body two-way communication, just putting a smile on your face for a few seconds or minutes, even forced, can make you feel better. Because the mind associates a smiling face with happiness, it will reason:

Hey, there is a smile on my face…I must be happy.

A study performed on depressed patients showed that after about 20 minutes of such "smile therapy," patients felt better (less depressed, happier). Therefore, put a smile on your face as you think positive thoughts and de-stress!

8) Any Combination Of #1-7:

You can take a walk on the beach, combining exercise (#6 above) and changing your environment (#5 above). In addition, you can practice deep breathing (#3 above). You can either stop for a few minutes to practice the Deep Breathing technique or practice as you walk along the beach.

So, a key to stopping the Stress Response is to engage in healthy activities that allow the mind to feel that the situation is not one of life or death, and therefore you do not need the Stress Response...it was a false alarm, and the SNS can be turned off.

Chapter 9: Tools of De-stressing Part Two - Recovering From Stress

Summary of Tools For Recovering From The Effects Of Falsely Activating The Stress Response:

1) Tools #2-7 As Described In Chapter 8.
2) Engage in healing-nurturing activities that stimulate the PSNS.
3) Yoga Exercise.
4) Deep Relaxation Exercise.
5) Deep Breathing Concentration Technique.

This section addresses a situation where you were not able to stop yourself from overreacting to a non-life-threatening situation or interrupt and stop the Stress Response early on by applying the techniques in Chapter 8, above. Therefore, the Stress Response was activated for an extended time.

In an appropriately activated Stress Response, that is, one where there is a real life or death situation, after the danger is over, the Nervous System would go into a recuperation period to balance itself and come back to normal. As previously discussed, it is the PSNS that counters the effects of the SNS. So, the recuperation period is the period between the SNS stopping the activation of the Stress Response and the PSNS restoring balance. The recuperation period is marked by tiredness and fatigue, due to the effects of the Stress Response on the mind-emotions and the physical body. It is the experience of how you would feel after having been through a real life or death situation. Having burned up so much energy to survive, and having been so tense, you would still feel shaky and anxious at first, and then exhausted, mentally-emotionally and physically. As you continued to feel that you were out of the danger and safe, the PSNS would continue to bring you back to your normal balance, until you *felt like your old self again*, so to speak.

When one is reacting to a situation that is not life or death as if it were life or death, the Stress Response will continue to be activated until something happens to interrupt one's response to the situation, such as the application of the tools discussed in this book. Even distraction and giving up on the situation are variations of the de-stressing techniques of changing the environment and changing one's thoughts, given above.

The key to recovering from a stress attack is to nurture yourself in ways that will evoke the PSNS response. So, the techniques given here are to nurture, heal, and restore energy and vitality, and stimulate the PSNS. The safer you make yourself feel, the sooner the SNS will shut down the Stress Response, so that the recuperation period can get underway.

> The key to recovering from a stress attack is to nurture yourself.

It would seem that as in a real life or death situation, this balancing should occur naturally, but in a real life or death situation, when you are out of danger, the Stress Response has accomplished its mission of saving your life, and its work is done, so it can cease and desist. However, because most people are used to overreacting in situations that are not life or death, but are more emotionally upsetting, they are usually not able to bring the situation to some final resolution, which would turn off the Stress Response. Usually, they continue to be upset about some aspect of the situation, such as the person involved, a resolution that they felt was unfair to them, facing the situation again in the future, etc., and so the fear and upset that initially triggered the situation does not resolve fully. There is also a tendency to mentally relive the situation, over and over again.

In addition, this overly emotional way of responding to non-life or death situations is a habit for many persons, so they frequently experience false alarm activations of the Stress Response. All this keeps the Stress Response simmering at a low level. Although the PSNS is able to exert some effect, it is also at a low level. In other words, the response of the PSNS is suppressed. Therefore, it is important to engage in practices that re-energize and vitalize the body and mind, as well as stimulate the PSNS, and shut off the Stress Response.

These de-stressing tools are also beneficial for healing and recuperating from activation of the Stress Response in true Life or Death situations.

1) Practice Techniques #2-7 As Described In Chapter 8:

You can practice any or all of tools #2-7, described in Chapter 8, because in addition to stopping the Stress Response, they can also facilitate the recuperation healing-balancing period. With respect to recovering from a false alarm triggering of the Stress Response, technique #2 in Chapter 8, *redirecting the thought process to the opposite thought*, should be practiced even if the incident is over. You should consciously correct your erroneous way of thinking. You can say something to yourself like:

> *Wow, that one really got away from me...I sure reacted to that situation as if it were a life or death crisis. It was a difficult situation, but it was not a life or death crisis. I could have spared myself all the stress, and just approached the situation as a difficult situation or as a challenge. As it was, I still had to deal with the situation, but I did not have to deal with it being all stressed out. My overreaction made a situation I found to be difficult even more difficult, plus now I am so*

drained. I am so tired and fatigued. All that drama was not necessary. I did not need to activate my Stress Response and drain myself of energy and vitality. Next time I will put forth effort to remain calm while I handle the difficulty. I will remind myself it is not a life or death situation. I certainly will be able to think more clearly, and likely not have regrets because I will not be saying the inappropriate things I tend to say when I am so upset.

This recognition and conscious acknowledgment will assist the process of breaking the old habit of overreacting.

2) Engage In Healing-Nurturing Activities That Stimulate The PSNS:

When you engage in nurturing activities that promote a sense of well-being and healing, signals are sent to stop the Stress Response. These activities signal the SNS that you are safe, and therefore, there is no need for its life or death response. The conversation goes something like this,

I must not be in danger since I am being nurtured...I must be safe...I can shut off the Stress Response and let the PSNS take over!

Some nurturing activities include a nice, warm candlelight bath, maybe with aromatherapy, perhaps after you have given yourself a massage with warmed massage oil; taking the time to prepare a nice healthy meal for yourself, and then sitting and eating it quietly; listening to soft, gentle music; or a combination of these as well as the de-stressing tools from Chapter 8. For example, you can set up an aromatherapy kit or light incense and candles in the area where you will practice the Deep Breathing technique.

Nurturing activities:

   a. Take a warm aromatherapy bath.

   b. Perform self-massage with warm oil, followed by a warm candlelit shower or bath.

   c. Slowly sip a cup of your favorite herbal tea in quiet surroundings. Chamomile herbal tea is noted for its relaxing properties.

d. Arrange a professional massage for yourself.

e. Prepare a healthy and tasty meal for yourself, and then sit down and eat it quietly (i.e., no TV; soft music is ok).

Stress and Overeating:

Although the Stress Response is associated with a decrease in appetite, the recuperation period is associated with the need to feel safe and nurtured. This need to nurture oneself and feel safe by eating can turn into overeating if the stress is not controlled or if it is ongoing. So eating a healthy meal also implies eating to moderation, i.e., not overeating.

If you find you are overeating, in addition to practicing de-stressing techniques, you should seek counseling from a dietitian and therapist to facilitate de-stressing in a balanced manner.

One of the signs of stress is going to extremes, so not eating enough or overeating can both be stress related. Also, eating can be a means of distracting oneself from one's worries and anxieties when one feels stressed, but it is not a healthy way of handling stress, as it can result in obesity, which can predispose to conditions such as diabetes.

3) Yoga Exercise:

Yoga Exercise is a very profound way to recuperate from activation of the Stress Response, i.e., stress. Yoga Exercise has a major effect on the Nervous System. It activates the PSNS, thus restoring vitality, energy and healing-balance.

Yoga counters the SR by activating the PSNS

Generally speaking, Western culture is plagued by the problem of sympathetic (SNS) overdrive. Thus, most of the population is stressed out and consequently, the PSNS is suppressed. Yoga[30], which includes Yoga Exercise, activates the PSNS, the calming-resting system, and therefore is an excellent way to de-stress[31].

Health Benefits of Yoga[32]:

The following are health benefits of Yoga that have been scientifically documented:

- Decreased Blood Pressure
- Decreased Anxiety
- Improvements in Patients with Angina Pectoris:
    - Improved Exercise Tolerance
    - Increased Maximum Workload
    - Delayed ECG Abnormalities During Exercise
    - Decreased Anxiety
    - Improved Relationships
- Decreased Need for Tranquillizers and Anti-Anginal Drugs
- Improved Sleeping Patterns
- Improved Personal Relationships
- Increased Skin Resistance (Lower Anxiety)
- Lower Heart Rate
- Lower Respiration
- Greater Alertness
- Enhanced Temperature Homeostasis

Therefore, as you can see, the health benefits of Yoga are equivalent to the functions of the PSNS in countering the Stress Response (SNS) [refer to Table 1: *Summary of Effects of the Sympathetic Nervous System (Stress Response) and the Parasympathetic Nervous System (counters Stress Response)*, at the end of Chapter 4, above]. Therefore, Yoga Exercise is a very effective tool to counter stress.

Additionally, the practice of Yoga Exercise has other benefits for the physical body and mind-emotions. It emphasizes Proper Breathing, Deep (Three-Part, Yogic) Breathing throughout the class, and Deep Relaxation (described in the next section below) is usually practiced at the end of the class to further promote de-stressing. Therefore, you will also gain the benefits of the deep breathing and deep relaxation on stimulating the PSNS and suppressing the SNS and the Stress Response[33]. The focus on deep breathing also prevents the body from being deprived of oxygen as occurs in many other types of exercises that cause the person to start panting as the body tries to get more oxygen to meet its deficit.

Exercises that cause oxygen deprivation enough to lead to panting and hyperventilating may burn calories, but they do not allow the body and mind to deeply relax because they mimic the Stress Response. Therefore, the Nervous System interprets the state of oxygen deficiency and the panting as if you were experiencing a life or death situation, because it would reason: *Why would I be in a state of oxygen deprivation if I were not in some dire circumstance?* So, after overly strenuous activities where one loses one's breath, such as jogging, after one catches one's breath, one experiences a lull in energy as the body goes through its recuperation and healing-balancing phase.

But in Yoga Exercise, there is a focus on deep breathing throughout the practice, so that a greater amount of oxygen than normal is breathed in to accommodate the exercise activity as well as cleanse the wastes and heal the body; thus, there is no oxygen deficit, and the Stress Response is not triggered. This explains the profound relaxation you feel after practicing Yoga Exercise. After the Yoga Exercise session, the body actually ends up oxygen rich, and therefore has more energy and vitality.

Because Yoga Exercise incorporates the Deep Breathing technique, after a session, the body actually ends up oxygen rich, and one feels energized.

Additional benefits of Yoga Exercise [34]/[35]:

- It balances the Endocrine/Hormonal System. In addition to the effects of the PSNS to balance these systems, specific movements and postures of Yoga Exercise massage and bring more blood circulation to the glands that produce the hormones (Endocrine System), thus balancing them, and all the other systems of the body (e.g., Immune, Cardiovascular, Gastrointestinal, etc.).

- Certain postures promote cleansing of the lymphatic system, which is described as the sewage system of the body, and is important for good immune function.

- The different postures and deep breathing massage the different internal organs and increase the blood circulation to them to keep them toned and healthy.

- It emphasizes alignment of the spine, tones the Nervous System and keeps the spine flexible.

- The gentle stretching in each posture releases the tension that accumulates in the muscle tissue due to stress.

These benefits all promote physical health, as well as a sense of wellbeing, i.e., mental-emotional health. Although you can take Yoga Exercise classes on an as needed basis when you find that you are stressed out or are becoming stressed out, you will derive greater benefit if you practice it regularly, anywhere from once or twice a week to daily, depending on how much stress you are experiencing in your life.

> Practice Yoga Exercise regularly for greater benefit.

You may practice with a Yoga Exercise video (DVD), however, it is best to begin by attending live classes, so the instructor can assist you to perform the postures properly, to maximize de-stressing and prevent injury.

> Start by taking a live Yoga Exercise class with a certified Yoga Exercise teacher.

Caution on Practicing Yoga Exercise If You have A Condition of Ill Health:

If you have conditions of ill health, consult with a certified Yoga Exercise instructor before starting your practice.

Some Yoga Exercise postures should not be practiced for certain conditions of ill health. For this reason, it is advised that you attend classes with a certified Yoga Exercise instructor in the beginning, rather than practicing by yourself using a video/DVD.

Also, be sure to speak to the certified Yoga Exercise instructor prior to attending or enrolling in the class to discuss any conditions of ill health you may have, including asthma and back or neck problems.

As with any other exercise program, it is advised that you seek the approval of your health care practitioner before starting a Yoga Exercise program.

Caution on choosing a Yoga Exercise class:

Most types of Yoga Exercise systems involve gentle stretching and deep breathing as you move in and out of various postures. There are many different schools of Yoga in the West that offer different styles of Yoga Exercise, with different areas of emphasis.

Pick a Yoga Exercise class that promotes deep breathing and gentle stretching.

Seek a class that offers gentle stretching and focuses on deep breathing and relaxation. Avoid classes that promote rigorous postures, are done in elevated temperatures, or promote panting/rapid breathing, jumping and other abrupt movements, as these are likely to relay a message of danger to the SNS and activate the Stress Response, defeating the purpose of practicing Yoga Exercise. So, find a class that is nurturing, with gentle stretching, slow and deliberate movements, and an emphasis on breathing deeply.

4) Deep Relaxation Exercise:

Like Yoga Exercise, Deep Relaxation is a very profound way to recuperate from activation of the Stress Response, i.e., stress. As stated above, it is usually practiced at the end of a Yoga Exercise session, so taking a Yoga Exercise class is also a good way to practice this technique. However, it can also be practiced by itself. There are many documented health benefits of Deep Relaxation techniques[36].

This technique puts the body and mind into a super-relaxed state. It is best performed lying down, but can also be performed sitting up. When it is performed lying down, the experience will be more powerful than in the seated position, because by lying down flat on your back, you are assuming a most vulnerable position, which will signal the SNS that there is absolutely no danger, and stimulate the PSNS.

> Practice the Deep Relaxation technique for a good night's sleep; it suppresses the SNS and the Stress Response and activates the PSNS.

You may become so relaxed that you fall asleep; your sleep will be very peaceful and deep. Thus, this technique can be used at bedtime (in your bed) to promote a good night's sleep. If you do not want to fall asleep, you can set an alarm, but you do not want to be jolted out of this state of relaxation. Therefore, set the alarm to play gentle, relaxing music. This entire deep relaxation should take about 15 – 20 minutes, unless you want to extend the final phase more than 5 – 10 minutes. Therefore, you can allow yourself ½ an hour on the alarm, just in case you drift off into sleep.

The Deep Relaxation Technique should be performed in a quiet, safe environment so you can feel comfortable closing your eyes. However, you can practice it with your eyes open if you are in a situation that does not permit you to close your eyes, such as at a conference or traveling on a bus or subway.

Deep Relaxation Technique –General Comments:

1) You can make an audiotape recording of the following instructions[15], so you can play it for yourself and follow the steps, step by step, as opposed to trying to practice and read it at the same time. Of course, if you do not have the capacity to make an audio recording, the latter will suffice, while you are either lying down or sitting up. However, once you become familiar with the technique, it is easy to recall, as you will be sequentially focusing on various body parts, from your toes to your head, and tensing and relaxing them.

2) Practice on a padded surface if you are lying down.

3) When you are sequentially lifting and tensing the various parts of the body in this exercise, be sure to observe how high off the floor you are lifting your body parts. You only want to lift the body part off the floor VERY slightly, ONLY about 2 inches. Most people overestimate the distance and lift the body part a lot more than 2 inches off the floor. Observe that you are not doing this, so that you do not hurt yourself by banging yourself when you release the body part back to the floor. You actually want to totally let go and just let the body part fall back to the floor with a little thud, and if it is only lifted off the floor about 2 inches, the release will not cause any injury or discomfort, especially that you are on a padded surface.

---

[15] Audio (DVD) instruction is also available form the author. See the catalog in the back of this book.

Practicing in a Seated Position:

The instructions below are given for practicing lying down. You may also practice in a seated position, such as if you are sitting at your desk at work. Be sure to keep your back straight. You can sit on a chair and place your feet flat on the floor, resting your hands on your lap. The most important point is that you are comfortable, and can be comfortable and not move or fidget in that position for the duration of the practice (15-20 minutes). When seated, it may not be possible for you to lift and tense some of your body parts; therefore, focus on tightening and releasing your muscles in these areas.

Deep Relaxation Technique - Part 1: Tense and Release

Step 1: Lay flat on your back, on a padded flat surface. You can place a cloth, towel or neck rest under the curve of your neck to support the neck. If you have back problems, placing a large cushion or pillow under your knees will support your lower back. Close your eyes.

Step 2: Spread your legs apart about 2 feet, and place your hands, palms upright, away from your sides about 1 foot (12 inches). Make whatever slight adjustments you need to make in your body to make it comfortable, and then keep it still, except as directed below. In other words, don't fidget after this point.

Step 3: Focus on your breath and breathe deeply. Inhale to the count of three (counting mentally). Exhale to the count of 3 (counting mentally). Over time, you can work up to inhaling and exhaling to the count of 6, without strain. Repeat 6 times consciously, and then allow the breath to continue flowing in and out, normally.

Step 4: Sequential Lifting, Tensing, And Releasing of the Body Parts (remember, only lift the body part off the floor VERY slightly, ONLY about 2 inches):

4-a: Now shift your attention to your left leg: Inhale and lift the left leg off the floor VERY slightly, and tense all the muscles in the left leg by squeezing them for approximately 2 seconds, then release the breath (exhale) and tension in the leg and let the leg drop back to the floor.

4-b: Repeat with the right leg.

4-c: Repeat with the buttocks, tensing and squeezing the muscles of the buttocks as you lift it ever so slightly off the floor, and then releasing the tension and lowering it back down to the floor with the exhalation.

4-d: Inhale and lift the left arm off the floor approximately 2 inches. Tense all the muscles in the left arm by squeezing them for about 2 seconds, making a tight fist, then releasing the fist and opening the hand. Next, release the breath (exhale) and all tension in the arm and let the arm drop back to the floor.

4-e: Repeat with the right arm.

4-f: Then shift your attention to the belly. Inhale and squeeze the muscles of the belly for about 1-2 seconds, then exhale and release (relax) them.

4-g: Repeat for the chest.

4-h: Focus on the muscles in your lower back. Inhale and tense them for about 1-2 seconds, then exhale and relax them.

4-i: Repeat for the muscles of the middle back.

4-j: Repeat for the muscles of the upper back.

4-k: Repeat for the muscles of the shoulders and neck.

4-l: Be aware that the entire body beneath the head is very relaxed at this point.

4-m: Focus your attention on the face. Inhale and squeeze all the muscles of the face together towards the nose for about 2 seconds, making a tight-prune face, and then exhale and release the tension. Now place a big smile on the face for few seconds, then release it and allow the face to relax comfortably.

4-n: Focus your attention on the scalp and release any tension there.

4-o: Note that the entire body is in a more relaxed state, as is the mind. Now we will move into deepening the relaxation.

Deep Relaxation Technique - Part 2: Relaxation Auto-suggestion

If you are pressed for time, you can perform Part 2 of the relaxatio n technique by itself

Note: If you are pressed for time, you can perform Part 2 of the Deep Relaxation technique by itself, but it will be more effective if you perform Part 1 before.

If you kept your eyes open in Part 1, close them now, unless your circumstances do not permit it.

Continue to lie or sit still and breathe deeply. Now you will sequentially focus on each part of the body and give it an autosuggestion to relax.

Step 5: Now bring your awareness to your left leg.

5-a: Focus your attention on your toes and mentally repeat, "My toes are relaxed."

5-b: Then shift your awareness to your foot, and mentally repeat, "My foot is relaxed."

5-c: Shift your attention to your ankle and calf, and mentally repeat, "My ankle and calf are relaxed."

5-d: Shift your attention to your knee, thigh and hip, and mentally repeat, "My knee, thigh and hip are relaxed."

5-e: Be aware that the entire left leg is now relaxed, and allow it to as if sink into the floor.

Step 6: Repeat this process (Step 5) for the right leg.

Step 7: Bring your awareness to your left arm.

7-a: Focus your attention on your fingers and mentally repeat, "My fingers are relaxed."

7-b: Then shift your awareness to your hand, and mentally repeat, "My hand is relaxed."

7-c: Shift your attention to your wrist and forearm, and mentally repeat, "My wrist and forearm are relaxed."

7-d: Shift your attention to your upper arm and shoulder, and mentally repeat, "My upper arm and shoulder are relaxed."

7-e: Be aware that the entire left arm is now relaxed, and allow it to as if sink into the floor.

Step 8: Repeat this process (Step 7) for the right arm.

Steps 9-20: Continue to focus on the various body parts, in the following order, mentally repeating the autosuggestion that each part is relaxed as you consciously focus your attention on it, and allowing it to as if sink into the floor:

Step 9: My buttocks is relaxed.

Step 10: My belly and all the organs and tissues inside the belly are relaxed.

Step 11: My chest and all the organs and tissues inside the chest are relaxed.

Step 12: My lower back is relaxed.

Step 13: My middle back is relaxed.

Step 14: My upper back is relaxed.

Step 15: My shoulders and neck are relaxed.

Step 16: My face is relaxed.

Step 17: My scalp is relaxed.

Step 18: And finally, even relax the breath, allowing it to gently flow in and out naturally.

Step 19: Now, allow the entire body to sink even deeper into relaxation, feeling as if it is sinking into the floor, as if the floor is completely supporting it, just as when you are floating on your back in a swimming pool or the ocean, you completely let go and let the water support you…so just let go completely and let the floor support the body, allowing it to be in a profound state of relaxation.

To keep the mind from wandering and promote a deeper level of relaxation, focus your attention on your breathing, observing the breathing in and the rising of the belly, and the breathing out and the falling of the belly. Remain in this deeply relaxed state for at least 5 to 10 minutes, and if your time permits, longer.

Deep Relaxation Technique - Part 3: Coming out of the Deep Relaxation:

Step 20: To come out of Deep Relaxation, proceed with slow and gentle movements as follows:

20-a: Gently roll your legs from side to side for a few seconds.

20-b: Then gently roll your arms from side to side for a few seconds.

20-c: Focus on your breathing and take a few deep breaths.

20-d: Gently roll your head and neck from side to side.

20-e: Slowly open your eyes.

20-f: Gently roll onto your left side, bend your knees slightly, and make a pillow with your arms and rest your head on your arms. Again, focus on your breath and breathe deeply for a few seconds.

20-g: When you feel ready to sit up, use your arms to support you and gently push yourself up to a sitting position. Remain there for up to a minute, allowing the body to come back into balance, being aware of your peaceful state of mind and body.

20-h: Move slowly as you stand up.

As you continue with your normal duties of life, this deep peace and relaxation will stay with you for some time.

5) The Deep Breathing Concentration[37] Technique

One way of unburdening the mind and bringing it to a deep state of rest and relaxation, which will also allow the physical body to release tension caused by stress, is to focus the mind and bring it to a point of concentration. This technique is enhanced by focusing the mind on a thought that is associated with peace and relaxation.

For most people, their minds are scattered and distracted most of the time; consequently, they are not concentrating their efforts on a particular task at hand. Psychologists say that as many as 80-90% of thoughts that people have are related to past occurrences/events, situations they cannot in any way change or alter because they have already occurred. Because many of these old and recycled thoughts relate to issues that have not been fully resolved on a mental-emotional level, these thoughts contribute to the low grade simmering of the Stress Response.

Deep Breathing Concentration is a profound way to relax the mind (and therefore the body also) while awake and alert. You will feel a release of tension and a sense of inner peace with practice.

When the mind becomes concentrated, it becomes relaxed, because it is not being bombarded by a lot of thoughts. Thus, focusing the mind on one thought is almost equivalent to the mind being thoughtless, i.e., without any thoughts, relatively speaking. A mind that can easily concentrate also becomes more effective and efficient, in effect, more powerful, and less susceptible to stress. Just think of how fast you accomplish a task when your mind is fully concentrated on it as opposed to when you are distracted with worry.

There are numerous documented health benefits of concentrating the mind. These include the same benefits detailed above for Yoga (see Chapter 9, #3: *Health Benefits of Yoga*)[38]. In his book, *The Mind-Body Effect*, Dr Herbert Benson, M.D., discusses that the mind-body complex has a counterpart response to the fight or flight response; he calls it the "relaxation response." He describes four specific behavioral practices and techniques that elicit this relaxation response: "a comfortable position; a quiet environment; repetition of a prayer, word, sound or phrase; adoption of a passive attitude when other thoughts come into consciousness.[39]" As you will note, the practice of the Deep Breathing Relaxation Technique described below incorporates all four of these elements, in addition to the added element of focusing on the movement of the abdomen. Therefore, you will experience considerable relaxation with the consistent practice of this technique.

Deep Breathing Concentration Technique[16]:

Choose a quiet environment or quiet time of the day, if possible, for your formal practice of this technique. It is best to practice this technique while sitting up, to minimize the likelihood of your falling asleep. Falling asleep would defeat the purpose of focusing or concentrating the mind, which allows it to rest and relax in a very deep and profound way.

You can sit on a chair and place your feet flat on the floor, resting your hands on your lap or in a crossed-legged position on the floor.

---

[16] Note: A guided Deep Breathing Concentration Technique CD is available from the author (see *Catalog* at the back of this book).

Be sure to keep your back straight. The most important point is that you are comfortable, and can be comfortable and not move or fidget in that position for the duration of the practice (20 minutes).

The foundation of this technique is the Deep Breathing technique you learned in Chapter 8. You will only add two steps as described below.

Deep Breathing Concentration Technique:

Step 1: Practice the Deep Breathing Technique

Practice for 5 to 7 rounds, or until you feel comfortable with the technique (as detailed in Chapter 8).

Then add the following 2 steps (Step 2 and Step 3):

Step 2: Coordination Of Your Breath And A Peaceful Thought Process

As you breathe in (inhale) and breathe out (exhale), you will enjoin a mental repetition of a word or short phrase that evokes peaceful feelings.

You may simply mentally repeat "peace" on both the inhalation and exhalation, or repeat "breathing in peace" on the inhalation and "breathing out peace" on the exhalation.

Alternatively, you can mentally repeat "breathing in peace" on the inhalation or in-breath, and "breathing out tension" on the exhalation or out-breath; with each exhalation feel that you are releasing more and more tension and becoming increasingly relaxed.

You can also choose to repeat a short prayer, mantra/hekau, or positive affirmation.

Whichever of the above concentration phrases you choose, stick to that one each time you practice. This will facilitate concentration and mental relaxation. If you use a different concentration phrase each time, this will only serve to distract the mind. Repetition (i.e., doing the same thing over and over again) is important when trying to engender a new habit.

Step 3: Focus of Attention (Awareness)

As you are breathing in (inhaling) and mentally repeating the peaceful concentration word or phrase (e.g., *I am breathing in peace*), focus your attention or awareness on the rising (ballooning out) of the belly. Then, as you are breathing out (exhaling) and mentally repeating the peaceful word or phrase (e.g., *I am breathing out peace {or tension}*), focus your attention on the deflation (falling or pulling in) of the belly. So, in addition to the repetition of the concentration word or phrase, the movement of the belly will be another point of focus to keep the mind from being distracted (i.e., to keep it concentrated).

Step 4: Bringing the Mind Back

Whenever the mind wanders, gently, without scolding yourself, bring your attention back to the coordination of the repetition of the peaceful word or phrase with the breath and movement of the abdomen. No matter how many times the mind wanders, each time gently guide it back to the synchronization of the focal points (repetition of the peaceful phrase, the breath, and the movement of the abdomen).

Additional Comments on the Deep Breathing Concentration Technique:

Practicing the Deep Breathing Concentration Technique will bestow peace of mind (relaxation) and an increased feeling of wellbeing. Further, with consistent practice, the mind will develop the ability to concentrate in a more effective manner. Practicing this technique will therefore increase your capacity to concentrate and be more efficient in other areas of your life, such as on your job.

If you are sitting in a cross-legged position and are not flexible or used to it, you may also experience leg cramps; you can gently open up your legs a bit, or move to sit in a chair.

At times, during the practice, you may feel sensations of lightness or floating, tingling in the legs or other body parts, involuntary twitching of facial or other muscles, or a tickling sensation of the skin, as if someone is lightly touching your skin with a feather. These sensations are not painful in any way, and are a normal part of the mind and body adjusting to the experience of relaxation and release of tension. Don't allow them to distract you from your practice. Just observe them in a detached manner if they arise, and continue with your practice.

Sometimes during the practice, you may become aware of a "lifting" or "release" of tension, as if its just melting away, followed by a profound experience of relaxation, inner peace and or joy.

However, even if you do not note any experiences or sensations during your practice, you are still benefiting; these experiences do not necessarily correlate to your experience of relaxation. To evaluate if you have benefited from the practice of this technique, consider how you feel at the end of this practice as compared to before the practice. If you feel more peaceful immediately after the practice than before, you have benefited. Even if your mind wandered during the practice, your peaceful feeling at the end of the practice indicates that your practice was still effective in relaxing and resting the mind. With continued practice, your capacity to concentrate the mind will increase, and the experience of inner peace and relaxation will become increasingly more profound.

This technique of Deep Breathing Concentration can be performed twice daily, in the morning and evening, 20 minutes each time, as a part of your daily routine to control the low-level ongoing simmering Stress Response resulting from anxieties, fear, or anger, as well as to release and recuperate from stress. However, if you find 20 minutes twice daily to be too challenging in the beginning, start with 5 or 10 minutes once or twice a day, and work up to 20 minutes twice a day over a period of weeks, months, or years.

This technique can also be performed as part of the Deep Relaxation Exercise described above in this chapter (#4). It can be incorporated at the end of Step 19 of the Deep Relaxation Exercise, when you focus your attention on the breath to keep the mind from wandering.

Chapter 10: Tools of De-stressing Part Three - Preventing Stress

Summary of De-stressing Tools To Prevent Becoming Stressed Out:

1) De-stressing tools from Chapters 8 and 9.
2) Right thinking followed by right action.
3) Making peace with death.
4) Finding a higher meaning in life.

The Unconscious Mind and Stress Response Activation

Applying the tools of de-stressing presented in this book will greatly reduce stress in your life. However, until the unconscious is cleansed of the old habit, which is a consolidation of years of wrong thinking and the nidus or seed that allowed the wrong thinking to develop in the first place, it won't be possible to be totally stress-free.

1) De-stressing Tools from Chapters 8 and 9

The de-stressing tools thus far presented will not only stop and or allow you to recuperate from stress attacks, but they will also make your mind less reactive in provocative situations. Thus, regular application of these tools, especially the Deep Breathing, Deep Breathing Concentration, Yoga Exercise, Deep Relaxation Exercise, and Deep Breathing Concentration techniques, will bring a profound balance to your nervous system, mind and emotions. You will find that you are not as easily triggered by circumstances that would have previously caused you to become stressed out. Thus, practice of these techniques over time will also have the effect of preventing you from becoming stressed out.

2) Right Thinking followed by Right Action:

Removing all possibility of ever becoming stressed requires cleansing the unconscious mind of the old habit of thinking wrongly about a situation (that it is a life threatening crisis), which leads to overreacting to the situation and becoming stressed out. This habit has become consolidated in the unconscious mind. This consolidated wrong thinking habit is cleansed in part by conscious right thinking that is followed by right action. This means following through on the conscious thought process about the situation not being one of life or death by not overreacting in situations that would normally cause you to become stressed out. Persistent right thinking (i.e., acknowledging that the situation is not a matter of life or death) followed by right actions (not overreacting) will eventually cleanse the old mental impressions and you will no longer feel impelled or compelled to overreact in non-life-threatening circumstances.

3) Making Peace With The Fact That You Will One Day Die:

To be really rid of the false activation of the Stress Response, there is one issue of life or death that must be resolved, that is, the fact that your physical body will one day die. This sense of mortality breeds a sense of vulnerability, which develops into an unconscious, and sometimes also a conscious, fear of death. The fear of death is a seed or nidus that must be cleansed from the unconscious mind to become totally stress-free.

You may feel that you are not afraid of death, but if you experience stress, you are experiencing fear of death. Consider why else would you react to a non-life or death situation as if it were a matter of life or death. Certainly not because you are afraid to live. No, because you are afraid to die. Consciously you may feel that you are not afraid to die, but by the fact that you become stressed out, your mind is demonstrating to you that it is telling you another story at a deeper level of mind, the unconscious mind. At the level of the unconscious mind, the incident that is stressing you out is registering as being a life-threatening situation for you.

Therefore, learning to conquer the fear of death and cleansing the unconscious mind of the fear of death is necessary in order to eliminate stress from one's life.

Given that everyone must one day die, fearing death is not a correct way to live life. It makes the whole process of living fear-based, whereby anything that one perceives as a threat to one's wellbeing can evoke a sense of being in a life or death situation, and activate the Stress Response. As discussed previously, if one is in a true life or death situation, then this may be an appropriate reaction. However, when one is not in a life or death situation, then it creates unnecessary stress. Therefore, not only does thinking about dying become stressful, but also living becomes stressful...there is no peace.

Accepting Death As A Normal Part Of Life

Because death of the physical body is a normal part of life, and because you know that your physical body will one day die, the main issue with death relative to becoming stressed out is not death itself, but fear of death. Unless you are actually in a life or death situation when you are having a fearful thought about dying, it is an overreaction...i.e., inappropriate stress. So, fear of death/dying can be a source of stress, and feeling stressed out. You should therefore apply the tools of de-stressing learned in Chapters 8 and 9 to mitigate the effects of stress you may experience when you consciously think about death, even as you work to correctly (fearlessly) think about death:

a. Recognize the signs of a stress attack.
b. Practice Deep Breathing.
c. Eat healthy meals...do not skip meals; vegetarian diet.
d. Change your environment...i.e., go for a walk.
e. Engage in light or moderate exercise.
f. Change your conscious thought process.
g. Engage in healing-nurturing.
h. Practice Yoga Exercise.
i. Practice Deep Relaxation exercise.
j. Practice Deep Breathing Concentration technique.

Think Correctly - Consciously Accept Death of The Physical Body As A Fact Of Life

The fact is that everyone will one day experience death of the physical body. All living things (non-human animals, trees, etc.) will one day die. Even inanimate objects die, because everything in the world will eventually degenerate and lose its current form. Scientists inform us that ultimately, even the sun will come to an end and the earth will cease to exist.

In some cultures, death of the physical body is treated and emphasized as a normal part of the process of human life, and is explored and discussed in normal day-to-day conversations, myths, rituals, philosophy and spirituality; all of this tends to minimize stress related to the unconscious fear of death, and may even lead individuals to overcome the fear of death altogether.

In many Western cultures, however, death of the physical body is not usually discussed on a regular basis in public or private conversations, and is ignored for the most part. Most people only discuss it if they have to because someone they know has died, and even then, it is usually an awkward conversation. Consequently, the emphasis in these cultures is on being youthful, vital and healthy, and not thinking about death. Yet, everyone faces old age, loss of strength, disease and death; this is part of the human journey, part of life. However, when some unexpected situation occurs, like the death of a friend or family member, individuals are shocked into facing the reality of death, but often do not know how. Many people become so distraught that they react as if they themselves are in a life or death situation, and become very stressed out.

Feeling stressed when you are thinking about getting old or becoming ill is another variation of the fear of death, because the fear in the mind is that if you become ill, you could die, and likewise getting old means that you are heading to eventual death. Yet, death is not reserved for the old or ill...it can also affect the young and healthy. In addition, you have probably had many bouts of illness from which you have recovered. You have seen or heard about friends or family who have been gravely ill, yet recovered. Therefore, illness does not necessarily equal death. Really, there is no knowing how long you will live. You may be all stressed out about getting old, yet may live a very long life relative to the human life span.

Consider that non-human animals also die, yet they do not spend their lives worrying about dying. This allows them to live each day anew, and sleep peacefully. In this respect, non-human animals experience a better quality of life than many human beings. The human animal, though possessing a higher consciousness than non-human animals, has cultivated a bad habit of fearing death. As explained above, fear of death is related to being stressed out. If you were not afraid of dying, you would not be reacting to non-life or death situations as if they were life or death situations and activating the Stress Response. So, the fear of death is an underlying factor when you are feeling stressed out, and therefore, it is something you should focus on countering on a daily basis, as part of de-stressing.

> Being stressed out is tied to an unconscious fear of death.

Therefore, whenever you consciously experience stress from thinking about getting old, becoming ill or dying, correct the thought process. Tell yourself something like:

Death of the physical body is a normal part of the cycle of life...just like being born and growing older. Not accepting that this body of mine will one day die does not make any sense. It would be like not accepting that a newborn child will grow up, that gravity exists, that the earth is round and rotates around the sun, that water is wet, or that the sun brings heat.

If you do not counter the thought process that death of the physical body is something to be feared, then you are essentially agreeing with these thoughts and creating a stronger impression in the unconscious mind that death should be feared, and this can keep agitating you in an unconscious way when you are not consciously thinking about it. This underlying agitation, because of the fear of death, can create a mental state where one is anxious and jittery for seemingly no reason at all. These pangs of anxiety and agitation may be experienced at times when you are not consciously thinking about death, so you may not be aware that this is the primary issue that is bothering you.

Some people feel that they fear death because they fear the unknown...they don't know what will happen to them after death. Yet, consider that each night when you consciously lie down and go to sleep, you leave the whole world behind as you enter into sleep. When you sleep, you are also facing an unknown situation, because you cannot control your dreams. In your dreams you go to unknown mental worlds and experience countless situations, some pleasurable and some fearful or painful. Also, there is no guarantee that you will wake up in the morning. Yet most people do not fear sleep as they do death. Therefore, fear of the unknown does not fully explain the fear of death that most people experience, which fuels being stressed out.

Moreover, instead of fearing sleep and feeling anxious about going to sleep, most people welcome sleep. Why? Because sleep is accepted as a natural and normal part of life, especially that it happens so regularly, every 24 hours, and that everyone experiences it. So, the habit of accepting sleep as a normal and natural process is well established in the unconscious mind for most people. Death, on the other hand, is not a daily personal experience. But due to the globalization of the world and the easy distribution of news from around the world, people are exposed to death via the media on a regular basis. If one has not resolved the issue of fear of death, this can be overwhelming, and can lead to one not allowing oneself to consciously think about it, or disconnecting one's emotions from one's conscious thoughts so as not to feel upset every time one sees images of or hears about death. However, this only further exacerbates the fear of death, because consciously suppressing one's thoughts or emotions does not block their effects at the unconscious level of mind, and therefore, is not the same as accepting death as a normal part of life.

Just as with the other tools of de-stressing, it will take time for this practice of consciously thinking about death of the physical body with calmness and acceptance to become established as a good habit. So, persevere with patience. This, in addition to the practice of not overreacting to non-life or death situations, will prepare the way for overcoming the unconscious impressions linking the natural process of death of the physical body with fear. You will note that thinking correctly about death will bring some immediate calm...the intensity varying with the degree of one's acceptance. In addition, you can seek counseling, psychological or and spiritual, to work through this issue of fear of death and to accept death of the physical body as a normal part of life.

The Fear of Death and Your Sense of Self

One's fear of death is not only about dying physically, but encompasses anything that threatens your sense of who you are...your sense of self. So, even someone disagreeing with your point of view can trigger a stress meltdown, because although they are not threatening you physically, they are threatening your point of view, which is tied to your perception of who you are (i.e., your sense of self)...and therefore the perception is the same as a life or death threat.

Anything that threatens one's sense of self can trigger the SR.

The more you identify your beliefs about life, religion, politics, etc., with your sense of self, with who you are at your very core, the more you will feel threatened when interacting with others with differing points of view; such interactions will likely result in your becoming stressed out from a false alarm activation the Stress Response. This ication of who you are at your very core with your feelings and beliefs is an expression of egoism, and the source of much stress in life. So, stress is linked to the fear of loss of self, and the greatest threat to this loss of self is death of the physical body.

Stress is linked to the fear of loss of self.

Philosophical and Spiritual Inquiry

But, if you are not your feelings and beliefs, then who are you? Obviously, you are not just a physical body. And, even with respect to your physical body, you can lose different parts of your physical body, and yet "you" can continue to be "you." So who are you really? What happens if you let go of identifying yourself with your feelings and beliefs…what will remain of you? What will remain of you if you let go of your egoism?

This process of inquiring as to who one is beyond one's body and mental concepts is a major undertaking…and falls into the realm of philosophical or spiritual inquiry. This subject is beyond the scope of this book, the focus of which is the basics of de-stressing. However, resolving this issue as well as one's fear of death are essential in order to completely cleanse the unconscious mind and free oneself from susceptibility to being stressed out.

These subjects, inquiring into who one is beyond one's body and self-concepts, removing egoism and conquering and cleansing the unconscious mind of the fear of death is dealt with in the second book in this series: *Happiness 101: The Course You Were Never Taught In School*[40].

4) Finding A Higher Meaning In Life:

Sometimes the source of one's stress is not that easy to pinpoint. Your life may be going fairly well, with just the usual ups and downs. Your income and lifestyle may allow you to sustain the basic needs of your body and mind, but still you may feel that something is missing, and you may find yourself feeling uneasy and discontented a lot of the time, for seemingly no reason. You may even be wealthy so that you do not have to work. But still, you feel that there is something missing in your life, and feel uneasy a lot of the time.

If you feel like you need to seek a higher meaning and purpose in life, it may be time for you to engage in a personal spiritual quest. This too has been scientifically documented to reduce the incidence of becoming stressed out and promote an enhanced sense of well being[41].

You can begin by reading books about different spiritual traditions, exploring healthy lifestyle options, attending seminars and workshops that incorporate spiritually based healing principles, and then when you find an authentic path of spirituality and self-knowledge that resonates with you, focus on that[42].

Chapter 11: Conclusion

Stress does not have to be a part of one's life, but even if it is a part of one's life, it certainly does not have to be at the intensity that it is prevalent in our society. According to Dr. Sandra McLanahan, M.D., the four major causes of disease are:

1) Cigarettes
2) Alcohol
3) Diet – too much food or not the right food (i.e., the incidence of breast cancer is higher in overweight women)
4) Stress

Dr. McLanahan further points out that the first three causes are also stress-related[43]. So, approaching non-life or death situations as if they were life or death situations can lead to conditions of ill-health where the situation can become one of life or death. This is a very important point. Stress due to a falsely activated Stress Response can eventually become a self-fulfilling reality. Reacting to situations that are not a matter of life or death as if they are can lead to one's premature death. One can have a heart attack, or a stroke from High Blood Pressure, etc. So taking the time to de-stress in a healthy manner may very well prevent a real life or death situation from occurring in your life due to stress.

In addition to possibly saving your life, the tools for de-stressing presented in this book will also allow you to have a better quality of life. You will be more relaxed, and therefore more cheerful and happy. You will be able to handle the difficult circumstances with more patience and poise, and will find that approaching difficult situations with such an attitude facilitates their resolution. You will have a greater capacity to make peace with the situation even if the resolution is not in your favor. With practice, most non-life-threatening situations will not trigger you to overreact automatically, or you will catch yourself right away if you do overreact. Thus, the feelings and signs of stress you experience will be reduced, controlled, and some may even disappear.

It will take time and self-effort to apply the tools of de-stressing presented here, but one thing is sure, if you don't apply yourself and practice the various techniques and exercises, you will not be able to reap their benefits. Considering how stress impacts one's mental-emotional state and physical health, and how much time the average person spends feeling stressed out, the time that is required to practice these techniques is far less. So, why not spend your time engaged in positive activities, de-stressing, rather than in negative behaviors that are self-destructive, or being ill or even dead?

Many people, due to the pressure they experience from being stressed out, feel that they cannot take 5, 10 or 20 minutes a day to de-stress, but they spend much more time than this being stressed out and non-productive. Therefore, taking a few minutes a day to apply the tools of de-stressing can actually "create" more time for you, and thus make you more effective and efficient in your life. In other words, you are freeing up time that you would otherwise spend being upset, non-productive and inefficient, i.e., stressed out.

> De-stressing can actually "create" more time for you.

Over the course of 24 hours, is it so unreasonable to take at least ½ hr, or even 1 hr, of that time to promote your health, wellbeing and healing? Don't you deserve that?

Yes, you do!

REFERENCE NOTES

[1](a) Maxia Dong, Wayne H. Giles, Vincent J. Felitti, Shanta R. Dube, Janice E. Williams, Daniel P. Chapman, and Robert F. Anda. Insights Into Causal Pathways for Ischemic Heart Disease: Adverse Childhood Experiences Study. Circulation, Sep 2004; 110: 1761 – 1766: **"The purpose of this study was to assess the relation of adverse childhood experiences (ACEs)...to the risk of ischemic** heart disease **(IHD)...The present analysis adds to the already abundant evidence that adverse childhood experiences, or ACEs, are major determinants of health problems in adulthood. The fact that all but one ACE increased the risk of IHD, when combined with our finding of a graded relation between the number of ACEs and risk of the** disease, **offers particularly compelling evidence that a tie can indeed be drawn between childhood experiences and the subsequent risk of IHD."**

(b) American Heart Association website: www.americanheart.org (type in the words "abused children" on their Search engine), Journal Report 09/20/2004, Child Health News, Published: Wednesday, 22-Sep-2004. *Abused or neglected children are more likely to develop heart disease as adults.* **"Previous research found that multiple childhood traumas indicate 'a disordered social environment, and stressful exposures that can negatively affect the developing brain as well as emotional and social well-being,' the researchers write. 'The chain of events begins with childhood exposure to abuse, neglect and household dysfunction, which lead to development of unpleasant affective states, depression, anger/hostility, as a result of long-term effect of physiological response to stress. Attempts to cope with these stresses may also lead to the adoption of risk behaviors, such as smoking, overeating and physical inactivity.' "**

[2] Matthews KA, Katholi CR, McCreath H, Whooley MA, Williams DR, Zhu S, Markovitz JH. Blood pressure reactivity to psychological stress predicts hypertension in the CARDIA study. Circulation. 2004 Jul 6;110(1):74-8. Epub 2004 Jun 21.

[3] Dr. Eliot credits a psychologist, Capt. Neil S. Hibler, as developing this list.

[4] Eliot, Robert S., M.D., Breo, Dennis L, *Is it Worth Dying For?: How To Make Stress Work For You – Not Against You.* Bantham Books, 1989, p. 196

[5] (a) Schwartz PJ, La Rovere MT, Vanoli E. Autonomic nervous system and sudden cardiac death. Experimental basis and clinical observations for post-myocardial infarction risk stratification. Circulation. 1992 Jan;85(1 Suppl):I77-91. Review: **"sympathetic activation can trigger malignant arrhythmias, whereas vagal activity may exert a protective effect."**

(b) American Heart Association website: www.americanheart.org (type in the words "stress and heart disease" on their Search engine).

[6] Matthews KA, Katholi CR, McCreath H, Whooley MA, Williams DR, Zhu S, Markovitz JH. Blood pressure reactivity to psychological stress predicts hypertension in the CARDIA study. Circulation. 2004 Jul 6;110(1):74-8. Epub 2004 Jun 21: *"Conclusions*— **Young adults who show a large BP response to psychological** stress **may be at risk for hypertension as they approach midlife."**

[7] (a) Rozanski A, Bairey CN, Krantz DS, Friedman J, Resser KJ, Morell M, Hilton-Chalfen S, Hestrin L, Bietendorf J, Berman DS. Mental stress and the induction of silent myocardial ischemia in patients with coronary artery disease. N Engl J Med. 1988 Apr 21;318(16):1005-12: **"Personally relevant mental stress may be an important precipitant of myocardial ischemia-- often silent--in patients with coronary artery disease."**

(b) American Heart Association website: www.americanheart.org (type in the word "stress" on their Search engine).

[8] Matthews KA, Katholi CR, McCreath H, Whooley MA, Williams DR, Zhu S, Markovitz JH. Blood pressure reactivity to psychological stress predicts hypertension in the CARDIA study. Circulation. 2004 Jul 6;110(1):74-8. Epub 2004 Jun 21: *"Conclusions*— **Young adults who show a large BP response to psychological** stress **may be at risk for hypertension as they approach midlife."**

[9] Sacks FM, Donner A, Castelli WP, Gronemeyer J, Pletka P, Margolius HS, Landsberg L, Kass EH. Effect of ingestion of meat on plasma cholesterol of vegetarians. JAMA. 1981 Aug 7;246(6):640-4.

[10] Ornish lifestyle modification program continues to produce impressive outcomes for CHD. Healthc Demand Dis Manag. 1997 Apr;3(4):59-61

[11] Ornish D, Scherwitz LW, Billings JH, Brown SE, Gould KL, Merritt TA, Sparler S, Armstrong WT, Ports TA, Kirkeeide RL, Hogeboom C, Brand RJ. Intensive lifestyle changes for reversal of coronary heart disease. JAMA. 1998 Dec 16;280(23):2001-7. Erratum in: JAMA 1999 Apr 21;281(15):1380.

[12] (a) Astin JA, Shapiro SL, Eisenberg DM, Forys KL. Mind-body medicine: state of the science, implications for practice. J Am Board Fam Pract. 2003 Mar-Apr;16(2):131-47. Review: **"The literature was reviewed to examine the efficacy of ... psychosocial-mind-body interventions, including <u>relaxation...there is considerable evidence of efficacy</u>...in the treatment of coronary artery disease (e.g., cardiac rehabilitation), headaches, insomnia, incontinence, chronic low back pain, disease and treatment-related symptoms of cancer, and improving postsurgical outcomes...moderate evidence of efficacy... in the areas of hypertension and arthritis."**

(b) Bastille JV, Gill-Body KM. A yoga-based exercise program for people with chronic poststroke hemiparesis. Phys Ther. 2004 Jan;84(1):33-48: **"The** results suggest that yoga may be beneficial to people who have had a stroke."

[13] www.pcrm.org, *Vegetarian diets* by the American Dietetic Association: www.eatright.com.

[14] Position statement from the American Dietetic Association website: www.eatright.com.

[15] *Vegetarian diets* by the American Dietetic Association: www.eatright.com

[16] Ornish D, Scherwitz LW, Billings JH, Brown SE, Gould KL, Merritt TA, Sparler S, Armstrong WT, Ports TA, Kirkeeide RL, Hogeboom C, Brand RJ. Intensive lifestyle changes for reversal of coronary heart disease. JAMA. 1998 Dec 16;280(23):2001-7. Erratum in: JAMA 1999 Apr 21;281(15):1380.

[17] Ornish lifestyle modification program continues to produce impressive outcomes for CHD. Healthc Demand Dis Manag. 1997 Apr;3(4):59-61

[18] Aldana SG, Whitmer WR, Greenlaw R, Avins AL, Salberg A, Barnhurst M, Fellingham G, Lipsenthal L. Cardiovascular risk reductions associated with aggressive lifestyle modification and cardiac rehabilitation. Heart Lung. 2003 Nov-Dec;32(6):374-82. **"CVD patients who choose to participate in the Ornish program can experience greater improvements in CVD risks than patients who choose to participate in traditional cardiac rehabilitation or no formal program."** (Note: CVD = Cardiovascular disease, i.e., heart disease)

[19] Willett WC. Diet and cancer: an evolving picture. JAMA. 2005 Jan 12;293(2):233-4: **"...a 1981 landmark report...estimated that 35% of US cancer deaths were attributable to dietary factors...Among the international correlations between dietary factors and various cancers, the relation between meat consumption and colon cancer has been the strongest...Positive associations with intake of red meat have been seen consistently in case-control studies..."**

[20] (a) Barnard ND, Cohen J, Jenkins DJ, Turner-McGrievy G, Gloede L, Jaster B, Seidl K, Green AA, Talpers S. A low-fat vegan diet improves glycemic control and cardiovascular risk factors in a randomized clinical trial in individuals with type 2 diabetes. Diabetes Care. 2006 Aug;29(8):1777-83

(b) www.pcrm.org: Physicians Committee for Responsible Medicine News Release Archive 2006: New Study Supports Major Change in Diet Treatment for Diabetes: **"A low-fat vegan diet treats type 2 diabetes more effectively than a standard diabetes diet and may be more effective than single-agent therapy with oral diabetes drugs, according to a study in the August issue of Diabetes Care, a journal published by the American Diabetes Association...Study participants on the low-fat vegan diet showed**

dramatic improvement in four disease markers: blood sugar control, cholesterol reduction, weight control, and kidney function."

[21] Ornish D, Weidner G, Fair WR, Marlin R, Pettengill EB, Raisin CJ, Dunn-Emke S, Crutchfield L, Jacobs FN, Barnard RJ, Aronson WJ, McCormac P, McKnight DJ, Fein JD, Dnistrian AM, Weinstein J, Ngo TH, Mendell NR, Carroll PR. Intensive lifestyle changes may affect the progression of prostate cancer. J Urol. 2005 Sep;174(3):1065-9; discussion 1069-70. **"Experimental group patients were prescribed an intensive lifestyle program that included a vegan diet....resulting in significant decreases in serum PSA and a lower likelihood of standard treatment....In addition, substantially decreased growth of LNCaP prostate cancer cells was seen when those cells were incubated in the presence of serum from those who made lifestyle changes...intensive changes in diet and lifestyle may beneficially affect the progression of early prostate cancer."**

[22] (a)Toobert DJ, Glasgow RE, Nettekoven LA, Brown JE. Behavioral and psychosocial effects of intensive lifestyle management for women with coronary heart disease. Patient Educ Couns. 1998 Nov;35(3):177-88.

(b) Ornish D, Scherwitz LW, Billings JH, Brown SE, Gould KL, Merritt TA, Sparler S, Armstrong WT, Ports TA, Kirkeeide RL, Hogeboom C, Brand RJ. Intensive lifestyle changes for reversal of coronary heart disease. JAMA. 1998 Dec 16;280(23):2001-7. Erratum in: JAMA 1999 Apr 21;281(15):1380.

(c) Schmidt, T. F. H., Wijga, A. H., Robra, Bernt-Peter, Müller, M. J., et al. Yoga training and *vegetarian* nutrition reduce cardiovascular risk factors in healthy Europeans. Homeostasis in Health and Disease, Vol 35(4-5), Nov 1994. pp. 209-225

[23] Sacks FM, Donner A, Castelli WP, Gronemeyer J, Pletka P, Margolius HS, Landsberg L, Kass EH. Effect of ingestion of meat on plasma cholesterol of vegetarians. JAMA. 1981 Aug 7;246(6):640-4.

[24] The Comparative Anatomy of Eating by Dr Milton Mills, M.D., http://www.vegsource.com/veg_faq/comparative.htm

[25] You can visit the PETA (People for the Ethical Treatment of Animals) website for details of the slaughtering process: www.peta.org (type in the word "slaughter" on their Search engine. But beware, it can be a bit gory (I know this firsthand...in my pre-veterinary animal science courses, I witnessed that the methods used were not always effective, and therefore the life and death struggle the animals faced was at times very prolonged...resulting in considerable activation of the Stress Response).

[26] Berton F, Vogel E, Belzung C., Modulation of mice anxiety in response to cat odor as a consequence of predators diet. Physiol Behav. 1998 Nov 15;65(2):247-54.

[27] Eliot, Robert S., M.D., Breo, Dennis L, *Is it Worth Dying For?: How To Make Stress Work For You – Not Against You.* Bantham Books, 1989.

[28] Books, audiotapes, DVD's by Dr Sandra McLanahan are available through Shakticom: www.shakticom.org; 1-800-476-1347.

[29] You should consult your health care provider before beginning any exercise program, especially if you have any health issues.

[30] The Practice of Yoga encompasses several techniques or disciplines, including Yoga Exercise, Concentration-Meditation, Three-Part Breathing as well as other breathing techniques, Prayer, Philosophical studies, Ethics, Mantra repetition, etc.

[31] (a) Michalsen A, Grossman P, Acil A, Langhorst J, Ludtke R, Esch T, Stefano GB, Dobos GJ. Rapid stress reduction and anxiolysis among distressed women as a consequence of a three-month intensive yoga program. Med Sci Monit. 2005 Dec;11(12):CR555-561. Epub 2005 Nov 24: **"Women suffering from mental distress...show significant improvements on measures of stress and psychological outcomes."**

(b) Bower JE, Woolery A, Sternlieb B, Garet D. Yoga for cancer patients and survivors. Cancer Control. 2005 Jul;12(3):165-71. Review: **"Nine studies...yielded modest improvements in sleep quality, mood, stress, cancer-related distress, cancer-related symptoms, and overall quality of life."**

(c) Bentler SE, Hartz AJ, Kuhn EM. Prospective observational study of treatments for unexplained chronic fatigue. J Clin Psychiatry. 2005 May;66(5):625-32: **"Yoga appeared to be most effective for subjects who did not have unclear thinking associated with the fatigue."**

(d) Saper RB, Eisenberg DM, Davis RB, Culpepper L, Phillips RS. Prevalence and patterns of adult yoga use in the United States: results of a national survey. Altern Ther Health Med. 2004 Mar-Apr;10(2):44-9. **"..an estimated 15.0 million American adults had used yoga.... Yoga was used for both wellness and specific health conditions often with perceived helpfulness and without expenditure."**

(e) Ray US, Mukhopadhyaya S, Purkayastha SS, Asnani V, Tomer OS, Prashad R, Thakur L, Selvamurthy W. Effect of yogic exercises on physical and mental health of young fellowship course trainees. Indian J Physiol Pharmacol. 2001 Jan;45(1):37-53: **"There was improvement in performance at submaximal level of exercise and in anaerobic threshold in the yoga group... There was improvement in various psychological parameters like reduction in anxiety and depression and a better mental function after yogic practices."**

[32] (a) ibid

(b) Herrick CM, Ainsworth AD. Invest in yourself. Yoga as a self-care strategy. Nurs Forum. 2000 Apr-Jun;35(2):32-6. Review: "The National Center for Complementary and Alternative Medicine...and a branch of the National Institute of Health, states that **"During the past eighty years, health professionals in India and the West have begun to investigate the therapeutic potential of yoga....research studies...have shown that a person can, indeed, learn to control such physiologic parameters as blood pressure, heart rate, respiratory function, metabolic rate, skin resistance, brain waves, body temperature, and many other bodily functions."**
[33] Brown RP, Gerberg PL. Sudarshan Kriya Yogic breathing in the treatment of stress, anxiety, and depression. Part II--clinical applications and guidelines. J Altern Complement Med. 2005 Aug;11(4):711-7

[34] McLanahan, Sandra A, M.D., Health, Yoga and Anatomy – DVD/VHS; Shakticom.org, 800-476-1347

[35] (a) Heriza, Nirmala *Dr. Yoga: Yoga For Health.* New York. Penguin 2004.

(b) McLanahan, Sandra A, M.D., McLanahan, David J. M.D., Surgery and Its Alternatives: How to Make The Right Choices for Your Health. Kensington Publishing Corporation, 2002.

[36] Astin JA, Shapiro SL, Eisenberg DM, Forys KL. Mind-body medicine: state of the science, implications for practice. J Am Board Fam Pract. 2003 Mar-Apr;16(2):131-47. Review: **"The literature was reviewed to examine the efficacy of ... psychosocial-mind-body interventions, including relaxation...there is considerable evidence of efficacy...in the treatment of coronary artery disease (eg, cardiac rehabilitation), headaches, insomnia, incontinence, chronic low back pain, disease and treatment-related symptoms of cancer, and improving postsurgical outcomes...moderate evidence of efficacy... in the areas of hypertension and arthritis."**

[37] Concentration is the process of rendering the mind one-pointed, that is, working to bring it to a single focus. Concentration is also the first stage of the Meditation Practice. Meditation begins when the mind actually achieves that sate of being one-pointed and can hold it for some time. So, Meditation is a deeper process than Concentration and is usually achieved after a long period of intensively practicing Concentration. Thus, when most people say they are meditating, it would be more accurate for them to say they are concentrating, but since Concentration is understood to be an aspect of Meditation, the term Meditation is generally used for both.

[38] There are many researches that document the health benefits of Meditation. Concentration is the first stage of the Meditation Practice. Thus, you can experience the health benefits of Meditation even as you practice the Concentration technique:

(a) WILCOX, G. G. Autonomic functioning in subjects practicing the Transcendental Meditation technique. School of Applied Psychology,

University of New South Wales, Sydney, New South Wales, Australia, 1973: **"Improved Resistance to Stress and Greater Autonomic Stability: Faster Habituation of Skin Resistance Response to Stressful Stimuli; Fewer Spontaneous Skin Resistance Responses."**

(b) SMITH, T. R. The Transcendental Meditation technique and skin resistance response to loud tones. Department of Psychology, Eastern Michigan University, Ypsilanti, Michigan, U.S.A., 1974: Improved Resistance to Stress and Greater Autonomic Stability: **"Faster Habituation of Skin Resistance Response to Stressful Stimuli."**

(c) WILLIAMS, P., and WEST, M. EEG responses to photic stimulation in persons experienced at meditation." *Electroencephalography and Clinical Neurophysiology* 39: 519-522, 1975: **"EEG Indications of Greater Alertness (in Response to Photic Stimulation)."**

(d) ROUTT, T. J. Low normal heart and respiration rates in individuals practicing the Transcendental Meditation technique. Department of Psychology, Huxley College of Environmental Studies, Western Washington State College, Bellingham, Washington, U.S.A., 1973: **"Increased Basal Skin Resistance during Transcendental Meditation. Maintenance of a Relaxed Style of Physiological Functioning outside the Practice of Transcendental Meditation: Lower Heart Rate; Lower Respiration Rate."**

(e) MCDONAGH, J. M., and EGENES, T. The Transcendental Meditation technique and temperature homeostasis. Department of Psychology, St. Mary's College, Notre Dame, Indiana, U.S.A., 1973: **"Enhanced Temperature Homeostasis: Faster Recovery of Normal Skin Temperature following Exertion."**

(f) WALLACE, R. K., et al. Decreased blood pressure in hypertensive subjects who practiced meditation. Supplement II to *Circulation* 45 and 46: 516 (Abstract), 1972: **"Improvements in Hypertensive Subjects: Decreased Blood Pressure."**

(g) BLACKWELL, B.; HANENSON, I. B.; BLOOMFIELD, S. S.; MAGENHEIM, H. G.; NIDICH, S. I.; and GARTSIDE, P. Effects of Transcendental Meditation on blood pressure: A controlled pilot experiment. *Psychosomatic Medicine* 37(1): 86 (Abstract), 1976: **"Improvements in Hypertensive Subjects: Decreased Blood Pressure; Decreased Anxiety."**

(h) SIMON, D. B.; OPARIL, S.; and KIMBALL, C. P. The Transcendental Meditation program and essential hypertension. Hypertension Clinic and Department of Psychiatry, Pritzker School of Medicine, University of Chicago, Chicago, Illinois, U.S.A., 1974: **"Improvements in Hypertensive Subjects: Decreased Blood Pressure. Improvements in Patients with Angina Pectoris: Improved Exercise Tolerance; Increased Maximum Workload; Delayed Appearance of Electrocardiographic Abnormalities during Exercise (Delayed Onset of ST Segment Depression); Decreased Double**

Product; Clinical Observations of Decreased Anxiety; Decreased Need for Tranquillizers and Anti-Anginal Drugs; Improved Sleeping Patterns; Improved Personal Relationships."

(i) ZAMARRA, J. W. ; BESSEGHINI, I.: and WITTENBERG, S. The effects of the Transcendental Meditation program on the exercise performance of patients with angina pectoris. Department of Medicine, State University of New York at Buffalo, New York, U.S.A., and Buffalo Veterans Administration Hospital, Buffalo, New York, U.S.A., 1975: **"Improvements in Patients with Angina Pectoris; Improved Exercise Tolerance; Increased Maximum Workload; Delayed Appearance of Electrocardiographic Abnormalities during Exercise (Delayed Onset of ST Segment Depression); Decreased Double Product; Clinical Observations of Decreased Anxiety; Decreased Need for Tranquillizers and Anti-Anginal Drugs; Improved Sleeping Patterns; Improved Personal Relationships."**

[39] Benson, Herbert M.D., The Mind/Body Effect; Simon and Schuster; 1979

[40] *Happiness 101: The Course You Were Never Taught in School; An Introduction to Yoga Philosophy.* Contact Sema Institute of Yoga 305-378-6253.

[41] Kennedy JE, Abbott RA, Rosenberg BS. Changes in spirituality and well-being in a retreat program for cardiac patients. Altern Ther Health Med. 2002 Jul-Aug;8(4):64-6, 68-70, 72-3: **"retreats included discussion and opportunities to experience healthy lifestyle options. Exercise, nutrition, stress management techniques, communication skills that enhance social support, and spiritual principles of healing were incorporated... Experiential practices included yoga, meditation, visualization, and prayer....Changes in spirituality were positively associated with increased well-being, meaning in life, confidence in handling problems, and decreased tendency to become angry."**

[42] Recommended reading, book by the same author of this one: *Happiness 101: Course You Were Never Taught in School; An Introduction to Yoga-Mystical Philosophy and Spirituality.* Contact Sema Institute of Yoga 305-378-6253.

[43] Books, audiotapes, DVD's by Dr Sandra McLanahan are available through Shakticom: www.shakticom.org; 1-800-476-1347.

BIBLIOGRAPHY

Ashby, Muata, Ashby, Karen, Dr., *Egyptian Yoga Exercise Workout Book*, Sema Institute of Yoga. ISBN: 1-884564-10-0

Ashby, Muata, Ashby, Karen, Dr., *Kemetic Diet, Food for Body, Mind and Soul*. Sema Institute of Yoga. ISBN: 1-884564-49-6

Benson, Herbert M.D., The Mind/Body Effect; Simon and Schuster; 1979.

Eliot, Robert S., M.D., *Is it Worth Dying For? : How To Make Stress Work For You – Not Against You*
Bantham Books, 1989.

Heriza, Nirmala, McLanahan, Sandra A, M.D., *Dr. Yoga: Yoga For Health*. New York. Penguin, 2004.

Marieb, Elaine N, Essentials of Human Anatomy and Physiology, 6th ed, Benjamin/Cummings Science Publishing; 2000.

McLanahan, Sandra A, M.D., Audiotapes on Health (available through Shakticom: www.shakticom.org; 1-800-476-1347).

McLanahan, Sandra A, M.D., McLanahan, David J. M.D., *Surgery and Its Alternatives: How to Make The Right Choices for Your Health*. Kensington Publishing Corporation, 2002.

Ornish, Dean, M.D., *Dr. Dean Ornish's Program for Reversing Heart Disease: The Only System Scientifically Proven to Reverse Heart Disease Without Drugs or Surgery*; Ivy Books; 1995.

RESOURCES:

Psychologists/Therapists

American Board of Professional Psychology (ABPP):
www.abpp.org 800-255-7792;
912-234-5477

American Psychotherapy Association:
http://www.americanpsychotherapy.com 800-205-9165

Psychology Today: www.psychologytoday.com

Suicide Hotline

National Suicide Hotlines USA: 800-784-2433; 800-273-8255; Deaf Hotline: 800-799-4TTY (4889)

Relationships & Parenting

Relationships: Preventative Relationship Enhancement
Program www.prepinc.com 800-366-0166; 303-759-9931

Parenting: Connect With Kids (CWK Network, Inc.)
www.connectwithkids.com, 1-888-598-5437

Parent Effectiveness Training: The Proven Program For
Raising Responsible Children (Paperback And Audio) by
Thomas Gordon. Available on amazon.com.

<u>Vegetarian Diet: Books, DVD's & Other Materials</u>

Physician's Committee for Responsible Medicine (PCRM): www.pcrm.org, 202-686-2210

American Dietetic Association
<u>www.eatright.org</u> (do a search for the word "vegetarian")

McDougall Wellness Center
www.drmcdougall@drmcdougall.com
800 941-7111 or 707-538-8609

The Food Revolution (John Robbins):
www.foodrevolution.org

Rave Diet: www.ravediet.com

PETA's GoVeg Campaign: www.goveg.com
757-622-PETA

North American Vegetarian Society (NAVS):
www.navs-online.org, 518-568-7970

Preventive Medicine Research Institute (Dr. Dean Ornish):
www.pmri.org 415-332-2525

Sema Institute of Yoga
Kemetic Diet: Food for Body Mind and Spirit
Available through the Sema Institute (305-378-2653
www.egyptianyoga.com) and www.amazon.com

Yoga Exercise: Classes in Your Area, Retreats, Vacations:

Satchidananda Ashram Yogaville
(They have certified Hatha Yoga teachers all over the world; also inquire about Yoga classes or programs for specific health conditions, such as **Cardiac Yoga**® for persons with heart conditions, etc.)
434-969-4829; 800-858-9642
http://www.yogaville.org

Sivananda Yoga
(They have certified Hatha Yoga teachers all over the world.); 845-434-6492; 530-272-9322
http://www.sivananda.org

Yoga Alliance
(They can provide information on certified Yoga teachers all over the world.);
877-964-2255 (toll free); 301-868-4700
http://www.yogaalliance.org/teacher_search.cfm

Yoga Research Foundation
(Hatha Yoga classes in Miami, FL USA); 305-666-2006;
http://www.yrf.org

Yogi Hari's Ashram (They have certified Hatha Yoga teachers all over the world; also classes in Miramar, FL USA); 1-800-964-2553
http://www.yogihari.com

Sema Institute of Yoga (Yoga classes based on an Ancient African Yoga system); 305-378-6253
www.egyptianyoga.com

INDEX

CATALOG

www.DiscoverInnerPeace.com

Lectures/Workshops: *Contact the author*
Phone/Fax: 305-378-6253

E-mail: DrKarenDjaAshby@aol.com

CD's by the author: $19.99 each + S & H

<u>Title</u>: **De-Stressing 101: Tools For Living A Stress Free Life CD**
- Guided Proper Breathing
- Guided Three Part Breathing Technique – Basic
- Guided Three Part Breathing Technique - Advanced
- Guided Deep Relaxation Technique
- Guided Breathing Concentration-Meditation Technique

<u>Title</u>: **De-Stressing 101: Tools For Living A Stress Free Life – Extended Guided Relaxation and Meditation**
- Extended Guided Deep Relaxation
- Extended Guided Deep Relaxation and Concentration-Meditation

Other Books by the Author:

Happiness 101: The Course You Were Never Taught in School - Call or visit website for price.

Egyptian Yoga Exercise Workout Book, Sema Institute of Yoga. ISBN: 1-884564-10-0 (co-author) - $21.95

Kemetic Diet, Food for Body, Mind and Soul. Sema Institute of Yoga. ISBN: 1-884564-49-6 (contributing author) - $28.95

ORDER FORM
Order Online at: www.DiscoverInnerPeace.com
Phone or Fax Inquiries or Orders: (305) 378-6253

- ❖ **Wholesale-Bookstores/Distributors**: Call for discount info.
- ❖ **Postal Orders**: Mail to address Below
- ❖ **E-mail** - Contact us: **DrKarenDjaAshby@aol.com**

Please send the following books and / or CD's.
ITEM   Quantity
_____   _____   Cost $_____
_____   _____   Cost $_____
_____   _____   Cost $_____
_____   _____   Cost $_____
Sales tax: Add 6.5% for Florida addresses .... $ _____
Shipping: $6.50 for first book and .50¢ for each additional $ _____
Shipping: $6.50 for first CD and .50¢ for each additional $ _____
(Note: S&H for books and CD's are separate)   Total $_____
Shipping: Outside US: E-mail order or call for estimate of shipping charges (Note: please **do not** send cc info via E-mail)
Note: Prices & Shipping Fees subject to Change

Name:_____
Ship to Address (Physical address preferred): _____
_____   Apt#:_____
City:_____ State:_____ Zip:_____
Phone #'s: (_____)_____ (_____)_____
E-mail address: _____

Payment: Money Order, Check or CC (Note: Do NOT send cash)
_____Check -Include Driver License #:_____
Credit card: _____ Visa   _____ MasterCard   _____ AMEX.
Card number:_____
Name on card:_____
Billing Address if different than above:_____
_____zip_____
Exp. date: (month)_____/(year)_____
PIN (CID) # _____ (last 3 numbers in the signature panel on VISA & MC, 4 numbers on the front of the card above cc info on Amex)
Signature of cardholder:_____ Date:_____

Mail Inquiries or Orders:
Sema Institute
P.O. Box 570459, Miami, Florida, 33257
Attn. De-stressing 101

55416502R00093

Made in the USA
Charleston, SC
26 April 2016